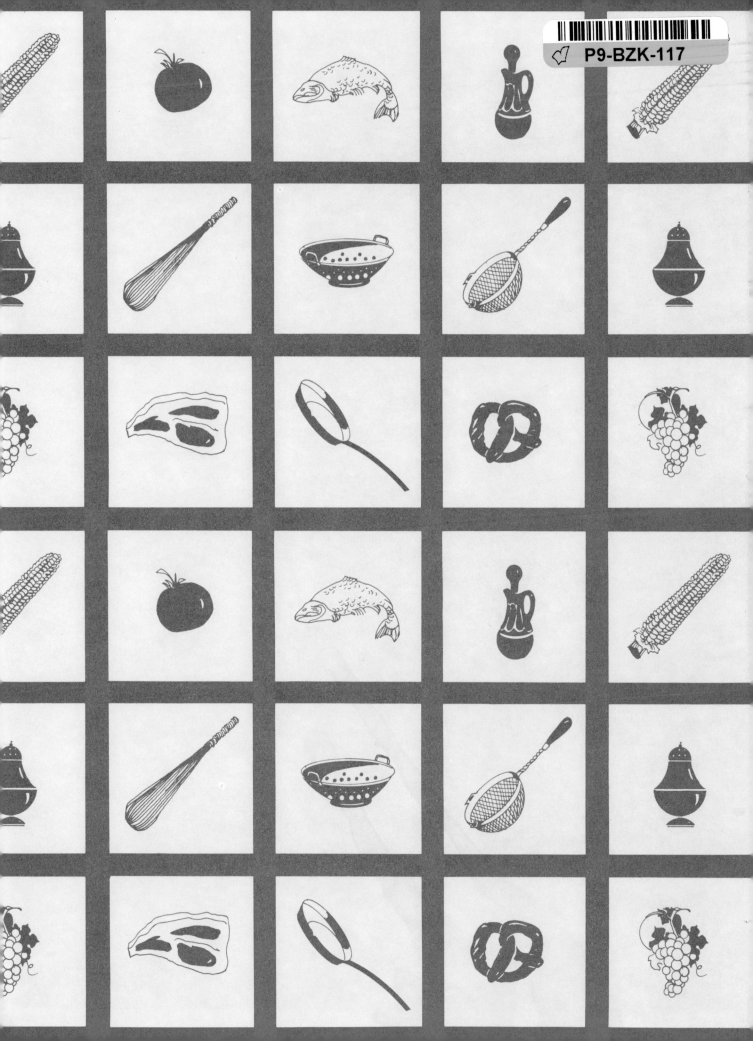

ILLUSTRATED LIBRARY OF COOKING

Cover photo: Austrian Boiled Beef *(Gekochtes Rindfleisch),* page 25

TIME LIFE BOOKS

ILLUSTRATED LIBRARY OF COOKING

Beef & Veal

Culinary Arts Institute®
A DIVISION OF DELAIR PUBLISHING COMPANY

Published, under agreement with Time-Life Books, by
Culinary Arts Institute
a division of
Delair Publishing Company, Inc.
420 Lexington Avenue
New York, New York 10170

The Time-Life Illustrated Library of Cooking
is a collection of tested recipes
by leading authorities in the world of cooking.
This volume contains recipes
by the experts listed below:

Michael Field, the consulting editor
for the Foods of the World series,
was one of America's top-ranking cooking experts
and a contributor to leading magazines.

James A. Beard, a renowned authority
on American cuisine, is also
an accomplished teacher and writer
of the culinary arts.

Allison Williams is the author
of *The Embassy Cookbook,*
her collection of authentic recipes
from various embassies in Washington.

ISBN: 0-8326-0808-4

Contents

Beef

Royal Pot Roast

Slottstek   *To serve 6 to 8*

2 tablespoons butter
2 tablespoons vegetable oil
4 pounds boneless beef: bottom round,
  rump, brisket or chuck roast
1 cup finely chopped onions
3 tablespoons flour
1 tablespoon dark corn syrup
2 tablespoons white vinegar
2 cups beef stock, fresh or canned
1 large bay leaf
6 flat anchovy fillets, washed and dried
1 teaspoon whole peppercorns, crushed
  and tied in cheesecloth
Salt
Freshly ground black pepper

1. Preheat the oven to 350°.
2. In a heavy 5- to 6-quart casserole equipped with a cover, melt the butter and oil over moderate heat.
3. When the foam subsides, add the meat and brown it on all sides; this should take at least 15 minutes. Remove the meat from the pan and set it aside.
4. Add the chopped onions to the casserole and let them cook over moderately high heat for 6 to 8 minutes, stirring occasionally, until they are lightly browned.
5. Remove the pan from the heat and add the flour. Stir gently to dissolve it, and then stir in the dark corn syrup, white vinegar and 2 cups of stock.
6. Add the bay leaf, anchovies and bag of peppercorns, replace the meat in the casserole, cover and bring to a boil on top of the stove.
7. Place the casserole in the lower third of the oven, regulating the heat so that the liquid in the casserole barely simmers. The meat should be tender in about 3 hours. To test, pierce it with the tip of a sharp knife: the roast should offer no resistance.
8. Transfer the pot roast to a heated platter and cover it lightly with foil to keep it warm.
9. Remove the bay leaf and bag of peppercorns from the casserole and discard them.
10. Skim off any surface fat and taste the remaining sauce; add salt and pepper if necessary. If the sauce seems to lack flavor, boil it briskly, uncovered, over high heat for a few minutes to reduce and concentrate it.
11. Pour into a heated sauceboat and serve with the meat. In Sweden *slottstek* is usually accompanied by red currant jelly or lingonberries, and often with gherkins and boiled potatoes.

Pot roast cooked in a covered casserole with wine, onions and carrots is tender and tasty whether served hot, as shown above, or cold *(page 13)*.

Pot Roast in Red Wine

Boeuf à la Mode   To serve 10 to 12

THE BEEF
1 tablespoon salt
1 teaspoon coarsely ground black pepper
A 5-pound boneless beef chuck or bottom
   round roast at least 5 inches in diameter,
   trimmed and tied
THE MARINADE
3 cups red Burgundy or other dry red wine
1 cup thinly sliced onions
¾ cup thinly sliced carrots
1 teaspoon finely chopped garlic
2 bay leaves, crumbled
2 tablespoons finely chopped fresh parsley
1 teaspoon dried thyme, crumbled

MARINATING THE BEEF: 1. Press 1 tablespoon of salt and 1 teaspoon of pepper into the surface of the beef.
2. In a large glass, porcelain or stainless-steel bowl, mix the marinade ingredients. Add the beef and turn it in the marinade until it is well moistened on all sides.
3. Let it marinate for at least 6 hours at room temperature or 12 to 24 hours in the refrigerator, turning it over every few hours.

THE ONIONS AND CARROTS À BRUN
½ pound fresh pork fat, diced
20 to 24 white onions, about 1 inch in
   diameter, peeled
6 to 8 carrots, peeled and cut into 1½-inch
   cylinders or olive shapes

THE ONIONS AND CARROTS À BRUN: 1. Preheat the oven to 350°.

2. In a heavy 10- to 12-inch skillet, sauté the diced pork fat over moderate heat, stirring constantly, until crisp and brown.

3. Remove the diced pork fat and reserve it.

4. In the fat left in the skillet, brown the whole onions and the carrots lightly over moderately high heat, shaking the pan occasionally to roll them around and color them as evenly as possible.

5. Transfer them to a shallow baking dish large enough to hold them in one layer, and sprinkle them with about 3 tablespoons of pork fat. (Set the skillet aside, without removing the remaining fat.)

6. Bake the onions and carrots uncovered on the middle shelf of the oven, turning and basting them once or twice, for 30 minutes, or until they are barely tender.

7. Remove from the oven, pour out the cooking fat and set the vegetables aside.

THE BRAISING STOCK
4 tablespoons butter
⅓ cup Cognac
2 calf's feet and/or 1 large veal knuckle, sawed into pieces
2 medium tomatoes, peeled, seeded and coarsely chopped
Bouquet garni **made of 6 parsley sprigs, 1 bay leaf and the white part of 1 leek, tied together**
3 cups beef stock, fresh or canned
Salt
Freshly ground black pepper
½ cup finely chopped fresh parsley

BRAISING THE BEEF: 1. While the vegetables bake or when they are done, remove the beef from the marinade and dry it thoroughly with paper towels.

2. Strain the marinade into a small bowl, and drain the vegetables on paper towels.

3. Heat the pork fat remaining in the skillet to the smoking point and brown the beef over moderate heat until it is richly colored on all sides.

4. While the beef is browning, melt 4 tablespoons of butter in a heavy, 6-quart heatproof casserole or Dutch oven.

5. Add the marinated vegetables and cook over low heat, turning frequently, until most of their moisture has boiled away and they are lightly colored.

6. When the beef is browned, use a bulb baster to draw off all but a thin film of fat from the skillet.

7. The next step is to flame the beef. Experts simply flame the beef with Cognac directly in the pan. But a more reliable way is to warm the Cognac first in a small saucepan over low heat, ignite it with a match, and pour it flaming over the beef a little at a time, shaking the skillet gently until the flames dies.

8. Transfer the beef to the casserole and surround it with the pieces of calf's feet and/or veal knuckle, the chopped tomatoes, the diced pork fat and the *bouquet garni*.

9. Pour the strained marinade and 3 cups of beef stock into the skillet, and bring them to a boil over high heat, stirring and scraping in any browned bits that cling to the pan.

10. Boil briskly for 1 or 2 minutes, then pour it into the casserole. The liquid should come about halfway up the side of the meat; add more beef stock if needed.

11. Bring the casserole to a boil on top of the stove, then cover tightly and place on the middle shelf of the oven. Regulate oven heat so the beef simmers slowly, and turn and baste the meat 2 or 3 times during the cooking.

12. After 2½ to 3 hours the meat should be tender when pierced with the tip of a sharp knife.

13. To serve the beef and the vegetables hot, transfer the beef from the casserole to a plate.

14. Remove and discard the bones and *bouquet garni* and strain the rest of the contents of the casserole through a large, fine sieve into a 3- to 4-quart saucepan, pressing down hard

on the vegetables before discarding them.

15. Let the strained braising liquid, or sauce, settle for a few minutes, then skim as much fat as possible from the surface.

16. Boil the sauce briskly over high heat until it has been reduced to half its original quantity (about 3 to 4 cups). Taste and season with salt and pepper.

17. Return the meat and sauce to the casserole and add the baked onions and carrots.

18. Simmer slowly on top of the stove to heat the beef and vegetables thoroughly.

19. Transfer the beef to a carving board to remove the strings. Then arrange the roast on a large heated platter, surrounded with the onions and carrots.

20. Spoon some of the sauce over it, and serve the rest separately in a warm sauceboat. lined with a dampened kitchen towel.

21. To serve the beef and the vegetables hot, transfer the beef from the casserole to a plate.

22. Remove and discard the bones and *bouquet garni* and strain the rest of the contents of the casserole through a large, fine sieve into a 3- to 4-quart saucepan, pressing down hard on the vegetables before discarding them.

23. Let the strianed braising liquid, or sauce, settle for a few minutes, then skim as much fat as possible from the surface.

24. Boil the sauce briskly over high heat until it has been reduced to half its original quantity (about 3 to 4 cups). Taste and season with salt and pepper.

25. Return the meat and sauce to the casseorle and add the baked onions and carrots.

26. Simmer slowly on top of the stove to heat the beef and vegetables thoroughly.

27. Transfer the beef to a carving board to remove the strings. Then arrange the roast on a large heated platter, surrounded with the onions and carrots.

28. Spoon some of the sauce over it, and

Pot roast is made into an elegant leftover by arranging slices with vegetables on aspic shapes and glazing it with more aspic.

To keep aspic chilled to the proper degree, work with the pan set in a larger container filled with ice.

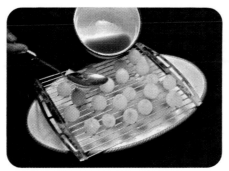

Vegetables to garnish are glazed with aspic that has been chilled almost to the point of thickening.

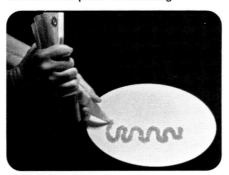

Aspic may be pressed through a pastry tube with a plain tip to produce scrolls or other designs.

Alternatively, aspic may be chilled more firmly in a shallow pan, then cut in diamond shapes or diced.

serve the rest separately in a warm sauceboat.

POT ROAST IN ASPIC
2 to 4 cups beef stock, fresh or canned
3 envelopes unflavored gelatin
3 egg whites
½ teaspoon lemon juice
½ teaspoon dried thyme, crumbled
½ bay leaf
10 peppercorns
1 teaspoon salt
½ cup dry Madeira

BOEUF À LA MODE EN GELÉE (cold pot roast of beef in aspic): 1. To prepare the cold version of *boeuf à la mode,* let the beef cool for an hour in the braising liquid, turning it once or twice.

2. Transfer the beef to a platter, let it cool to room temperature, then wrap and refrigerate it.

3. Strain the braising liquid; cool, cover and refrigerate it.

4. Cool, cover and refrigerate the baked onions and carrots.

5. When the braising liquid is thoroughly chilled, carefully remove and discard all of the fat that has solidified on the surface.

6. In a 2- or 3-quart saucepan, melt the braising liquid over low heat then measure it.

7. Add enough beef stock to make 5 cups in all, and return it to the pan.

8. Soften the gelatin in an additional 1 cup of cold fresh stock, and add it.

9. Beat the egg whites to a froth with a wire whisk, and stir them into the stock, together with the lemon juice, thyme, bay leaf, peppercorns and salt.

10. Bring to a boil over moderate heat, stirring constantly.

11. When the aspic begins to froth and rise, remove the pan from the heat. Let it rest off the heat for 5 minutes, then strain it into a deep bowl through a fine sieve lined with

(continued on next page)

a dampened kitchen towel.

12. Allow the aspic to drain without disturbing it at any point. When it has drained completely through, add the Madeira, and taste and season the aspic with more salt if needed.

13. Pour a thin layer of aspic – about ⅛ inch thick – into the bottom of a large serving platter, and refrigerate it until the aspic is set.

14. Then carve the cold beef into ¼-inch slices and arrange the meat, onions and carrots attractively on the platter.

15. Heat about ¾ cup of the aspic in a small pan just until it melts, then set in a bowl filled with crushed ice or ice cubes immersed in water.

16. Stir in the aspic gently with a metal spoon until it thickens almost to the point of setting.

17. Working quickly, spread a thin glaze of aspic over the sliced beef and vegetables. Chill until the aspic sets. Repeat this process two more times to make three coatings of aspic – melting and chilling for each layer.

18. Refrigerate the platter until the glaze is firm.

19. Meanwhile, melt the remaining aspic and pour it into a large flat roasting pan to make a sheet or film no more than ¼ inch deep; chill it.

20. When all the aspic is very firm, remove the roasting pan from the refrigerator, and score the sheet of aspic into diamonds with the tip of a sharp knife by cutting crossing diagonal lines about 1 to 1½ inches apart.

21. Arrange the diamonds on a platter and place the beef slices on top.

22. Dice the remaining aspic and garnish the platter with it as fancifully as you like. You can even put the chopped aspic into a pastry bag with a plain tip and press the aspic out in scrolls on the beef.

Standing Rib Roast with Yorkshire Pudding

To serve 6 to 8

An 8-pound standing 3-rib roast

1. Preheat the oven to 450° (it will take about 15 minutes for most ovens to reach this temperature). For the most predictable results, insert a meat thermometer into the thickest part of the beef, being careful not to let the tip of the thermometer touch any fat or bone.

2. Place the beef, fat side up, in a large shallow roasting pan. (It is unnecessary to use a rack, since the ribs of the roast form a natural rack.)

3. Roast the beef undisturbed in the middle of the oven for 20 minutes. Reduce the heat to 325° and continue to roast, without basting, for about 90 minutes, or until the beef is cooked to your taste. A meat thermometer will register 130° to 140° when the beef is rare, 150° to 160° when medium, and 160° to 170° when it is well done. If you are not using a thermometer, start timing the roast after you reduce the heat to 325°. You can estimate approximately 12 minutes per pound for rare beef, 15 minutes per pound for medium, and 20 minutes per pound for well done.

4. Transfer the beef to a heated platter and let it rest for at least 15 minutes for easier carving.

5. If you plan to accompany the beef with Yorkshire pudding *(recipe below),* increase the oven heat to 400° as soon as the beef is cooked.

6. Transfer the roast from the oven to a heated platter, drape foil loosely over it, and set aside in a warm place while the pudding bakes. If you have two ovens, time the pudding to finish cooking during the 15 minutes that the roast rests.

7. To carve, first remove a thin slice of beef from the large end of the roast so that it will

stand firmly on this end. Insert a large fork below the top rib and carve slices of beef from the top, separating each slice from the bones as you proceed.

8. Serve with its own juice and a horseradish sauce (page 25).

YORKSHIRE PUDDING
2 eggs
½ teaspoon salt
1 cup all-purpose flour
1 cup milk
**2 tablespoons roast beef drippings, or
   substitute 2 tablespoons lard**

1. To make the batter in a blender, combine the eggs, salt, flour and milk in the blender jar, and blend at high speed for 2 or 3 seconds.

2. Turn off the machine, scrape down the sides of the jar, and blend again for 40 seconds. (To make the batter by hand, beat the eggs and salt with a whisk or a rotary or electric beater until frothy. Slowly add the flour, beating constantly. Then pour in the milk in a thin stream and beat until the mixture is smooth and creamy.)

3. Refrigerate for at least 1 hour.

4. Preheat the oven to 400°.

5. In a 10-by-15-by-2½-inch roasting pan, heat the fat over moderate heat until it splutters.

6. Briefly beat the batter again and pour it in the pan.

7. Bake in the middle of the oven for 15 minutes, reduce the heat to 375°, and bake for 15 minutes longer, or until the pudding has risen over the top of the pan and is crisp and brown.

8. With a sharp knife, divide the pudding into portions, and serve immediately.

Beef in Beer

To serve 4 to 6

2 tablespoons flour
Salt
Pepper
2 pounds round beef in 1 piece
3 tablespoons butter
1 large clove garlic, crushed
1 large yellow onion, sliced
1½ cups beer
½ cup water
1 sprig parsley
1 sprig thyme, or a pinch of dried thyme
1 stalk celery
1 bay leaf

1. Pound 2 tablespoons of flour, seasoned with salt and pepper, into all sides of the beef with a wooden mallet.

2. Heat 1 tablespoon of the butter in a heavy skillet and brown the meat quickly on all sides. Remove the meat.

3. Put the remaining 2 tablespoons of butter into the pan and sauté 1 crushed clove of garlic and 1 sliced yellow onion until lightly browned.

4. Pour 1½ cups of beer and ½ cup of water into the pan and bring to a boil.

5. Replace the meat and lower the heat to simmering.

6. Put a sprig of parsley, a sprig of thyme, a stalk of celery and a bay leaf in the pan.

7. Simmer, covered, for about 1¼ hours, until the meat is tender.

8. Remove the meat and cut into serving pieces. Arrange on a hot platter and strain the sauce over it.

Marinated Pot Roast

Sauerbraten   *To serve 6 to 8*

½ cup dry red wine
½ cup red wine vinegar
2 cups cold water
1 medium-sized onion, peeled and thinly
   sliced
5 black peppercorns and 4 whole juniper
   berries coarsely crushed with a mortar
   and pestle
2 small bay leaves
1 teaspoon salt
4 pounds boneless beef roast, preferably
   top or bottom round or rump, trimmed of
   fat
3 tablespoons lard
½ cup finely chopped onions
½ cup finely chopped carrots
¼ cup finely chopped celery
2 tablespoons flour
½ cup water
½ cup gingersnap or honey-cake crumbs

1. In a 2- to 3-quart saucepan, combine the wine, vinegar, water, sliced onion, crushed peppercorns and juniper berries, bay leaves and salt.

2. Bring this marinade to a boil over high heat, then remove it from the heat and let it cool to room temperature.

3. Place the beef in a deep crock or a deep stainless-steel or enameled pot just large enough to hold it comfortably and pour the marinade over it. The marinade should come at least halfway up the sides of the meat; if necessary, add more wine.

4. Turn the meat in the marinade to moisten it on all sides. Then cover the pan tightly with foil or plastic wrap and refrigerate for 2 to 3 days, turning the meat over at least twice a day.

5. Remove the meat from the marinade and pat it completely dry with paper towels.

6. Strain the marinade through a fine sieve set over a bowl and reserve the liquid. Discard the spices and onions.

7. In a heavy 5-quart heatproof casserole, melt the lard over high heat until it begins to splutter.

8. Add the meat and brown it on all sides, turning it frequently and regulating the heat so that it browns deeply and evenly without burning. This should take about 15 minutes.

9. Transfer the meat to a platter and pour off and discard all but about 2 tablespoons of the fat from the casserole.

10. Add the chopped onions, carrots and celery to the fat in the casserole and cook them over moderate heat, stirring frequently, for 5 to 8 minutes, or until they are soft and light brown.

11. Sprinkle 2 tablespoons of flour over the vegetables and cook, stirring constantly, for 2 or 3 minutes longer, or until the flour begins to color.

12. Pour in 2 cups of the reserved marinade and ½ cup of water and bring to a boil over high heat.

13. Return the meat to the casserole. Cover tightly and simmer over low heat for 2 hours, or until the meat shows no resistance when pierced with the tip of a sharp knife.

14. Transfer the meat to a heated platter and cover it with aluminum foil to keep it warm while you make the sauce.

15. Pour the liquid left in the casserole into a large measuring cup and skim the fat from the surface. You will need 2½ cups of liquid for the sauce. If you have more, boil it briskly over high heat until it is reduced to that amount; if you have less, add some of the reserved marinade.

16. Combine the liquid and the gingersnap or honey-cake crumbs in a small saucepan, and cook over moderate heat, stirring frequently, for 10 minutes. The crumbs will disintegrate in the sauce and thicken it slightly.

17. Strain the sauce through a fine sieve, pressing down hard with a wooden spoon to force as much of the vegetables and crumbs through as possible.

A tenderizing and flavoring marinade of wine, onions, bay leaves, juniper berries and pepper transforms a boneless beef roast into savory *Sauerbraten*.

18. Return the sauce to the pan, taste for seasoning and let it simmer over a low heat until ready to serve.

19. To serve, carve the meat into ¼-inch-thick slices, arrange them in overlapping layers on a heated platter, and moisten with a few tablespoons of the sauce.

20. Pass the remaining sauce separately in a sauceboat.

NOTE: If you prefer, you may cook the *Sauerbraten* in the oven rather than on top of the stove. Bring the casserole to a boil over high heat, cover tightly and cook in a preheated 350° oven for about 2 hours.

Venezuelan Pot Roast

Asado Antiguo a la Venezolana Mechado   To serve 8 to 10

6 to 8 strips larding pork, cut ⅛ inch wide
   and 2 inches longer than length of the
   meat
4 pounds bottom round of beef, in one
   piece
3 tablespoons capers, drained and rinsed
2 tablespoons white distilled vinegar
¼ cup finely grated onions
½ teaspoon finely chopped garlic
1 teaspoon salt
¼ teaspoon freshly ground black pepper
¼ cup olive oil
1 tablespoon dark brown sugar
2 cups water

1. Lard the beef in the following fashion: Chill the pork strips in the freezer for 10 minutes or so to stiffen them.

2. First make a hole by inserting the point of the larding needle 2 inches into one short end of the meat; pull the needle back an inch or so and lay a pork strip in its groove. Then gradually force the needle through the length of the beef roast until the pork strip emerges from the other end.

3. Pressing the end of the strip where it entered the meat, carefully pull out the needle, leaving the pork in the meat. Repeat with the rest of the pork strips, spacing them at about 2-inch intervals.

A Venezuelan larded pot roast, shown with a plantain-and-cheese cake *(center)*, gets its distinctive flavor from capers, garlic, vinegar and brown sugar.

4. Trim off the protruding ends of the larding strips. Then, with the tip of a small skewer or knife, push one caper at a time into the beef around the strips of pork at both ends.

5. Combine the vinegar, grated onion, garlic, salt and pepper, and press and rub the mixture firmly into the outside surfaces of the beef.

6. Cover with foil, and let it stand at room temperature for at least 6 hours – or overnight in the refrigerator.

7. When you are ready to cook the meat, heat the olive oil over high heat in a heavy 4- to 6-quart casserole until a light haze forms above it.

8. Then sprinkle the meat evenly with the dark brown sugar and press the sugar into the meat with the fingers. Place the meat in the pot.

9. Regulate the heat so that the meat colors quickly and evenly without burning, turning it every few minutes to brown it on all sides.

10. When the meat is a deep-mahogany color, pour the water into the pan and bring it to a boil, scraping up any brown sediment clinging to the bottom and sides of the pan.

11. Cover the casserole tightly, reduce the heat to its lowest point and simmer the meat for about 2 hours, or until it shows no resistance when pierced with the tip of a small, sharp knife.

12. To serve, remove the meat from the casserole and carve it against the grain into neat $1/4$-inch slices, each of which should be patterned with tiny bits of larding pork.

13. Arrange the slices on a heated platter and cover it with foil to keep the meat warm.

14. Bring the cooking liquid in the casserole to a vigorous boil and cook it rapidly, uncovered, until it thickens to the desired consistency.

15. Taste the sauce for seasoning and either pour it over the sliced meat or serve it separately.

Braised Beef with White Wine

Manzo alla Sarda   *To serve 6 to 8*

MARINADE
3 cups dry white wine
¼ cup olive oil
¼ cup finely chopped parsley, preferably the flat-leaf Italian type
1 bay leaf, crumbled
⅛ teaspoon ground allspice
⅛ teaspoon ground nutmeg
1 tablespoon salt
A 4-pound boneless beef chuck or bottom round roast at least 4 inches in diameter, trimmed, rolled and tied securely in 3 or 4 places
2 tablespoons butter
2 tablespoons olive oil
1 cup dry white wine
2 cups beef stock, fresh or canned
2 tablespoons finely chopped fresh parsley
1 flat anchovy fillet, drained, rinsed and finely chopped
½ teaspoon lemon juice
Salt
Freshly ground black pepper

1. In a large glass, porcelain or stainless-steel bowl, combine the 3 cups of white wine, ¼ cup of olive oil, ¼ cup of finely chopped parsley, bay leaf, ground allspice and nutmeg, and salt.

2. Place the rolled and securely tied beef in the mixing bowl and turn it over in the marinade until it has become thoroughly moistened on all sides.

3. Marinate the beef for at least 6 hours at room temperature or for about 12 hours in the refrigerator, turning the beef occasionally.

4. Preheat the oven to 350°.

5. Remove the beef from the marinade and pat it completely dry with paper towels, but do not discard the marinade; set it aside to be used again later.

6. Over moderately high heat, melt the but-ter with the oil in a heatproof casserole that is just large enough to hold the beef comfortably. When the foam subsides, add the beef and brown it on all sides, turning it with 2 wooden spoons.

7. Transfer the browned meat to a plate and discard all but a thin film of the browned fat from the casserole.

8. Pour in the marinade and boil it briskly over high heat until it has reduced to about 1 cup, meanwhile using a wooden spoon or rubber spatula to scrape in any browned bits clinging to the bottom and sides of the pan.

9. Return the beef to the casserole and add 1 cup of white wine and the 2 cups of beef stock. The combined liquid should come about ⅓ of the way up the side of the meat; add more beef stock if necessary.

10. Bring the casserole to a boil over high heat, cover, and place in the middle of the oven.

11. Braise the beef for 2 to 2½ hours, turning it over in the casserole 2 or 3 times.

12. When it is tender enough to be easily pierced with the tip of a sharp knife, transfer the roast to a cutting board.

13. Pour the braising liquid through a fine sieve into a 1½- to 2-quart saucepan. Let it settle for a minute or so, then with a large spoon skim off as much surface fat as possible.

14. Boil the braising liquid briskly over high heat, stirring occasionally, until it has reduced to about 2 cups.

15. Stir in 2 tablespoons of finely chopped parsley, the chopped anchovy and lemon juice.

16. Taste the sauce and season it with salt and pepper if needed.

17. Cut the strings off the beef and carve the roast into thin, even slices.

18. Arrange the slices of beef, slightly overlapping, in a row on a heated platter. Moisten them with a few tablespoons of the hot sauce and pass the rest separately, in a sauceboat.

Braised Beef

To serve 4

1½ pounds top sirloin of beef
3 tablespoons butter
3 tablespoons sherry
1 clove garlic, crushed
1 teaspoon meat glaze
3 teaspoons potato flour
1½ cups stock
1 bay leaf
1 sprig tarragon, or a pinch of dried
  tarragon
Salt
Pepper

1. Trim most of the fat off the meat.
2. Brown quickly on both sides in 1 table-spoon of hot butter.
3. Heat 3 tablespoons of sherry in a small pan, ignite, and pour over the meat. Remove the meat from the pan.
4. To the pan add the clove of crushed garlic and the remaining 2 tablespoons of butter and cook about 1 minute.
5. Blend in, off the fire, 1 teaspoon of meat glaze, then 3 teaspoons of potato flour.
6. Pour in 1½ cups of stock and stir over the fire until the mixture comes to a boil.

7. Put back the meat with a bay leaf and a sprig of tarragon. Season well.
8. Cover and simmer for 1 to 1¼ hours, or until the meat is tender.
9. Remove and serve cut into slices with the gravy strained over it. Garnish with French fried potatoes (*recipe below*).

FRENCH FRIED POTATOES
4 or 5 old potatoes
Vegetable shortening or salad oil for deep-
  fat frying
Salt

1. Peel the potatoes and cut them into long thin fingers (one of the special cutters for French fried potatoes will save time).
2. Soak the cut potatoes for ½ hour in cold water. Drain and dry thoroughly on a cloth.
3. Cook until soft and lightly browned in deep hot fat at 370°. Drain on absorbent paper.
4. Just before serving, brown quickly in very hot fat at 390°
5. Drain again, sprinkle with salt and serve immediately. This double frying ensures complete cooking and crisp potatoes; with just one frying they may be half raw and limp.

The traditional New England boiled dinner is a hearty platter of corned beef and cabbage with other vegetables – carrots, beets, potatoes.

New England Boiled Dinner

To serve 6

4 pounds corned beef
2 pounds green cabbage, cored and quartered
12 to 16 new potatoes, about 1½ inches in diameter, peeled
6 small carrots, scraped
12 small white onions, about 1 inch in diameter, peeled and trimmed
6 medium-sized beets
2 tablespoons finely chopped parsley

1. Before cooking the corned beef, ask your butcher whether it should be soaked in water to remove some of the salt. If it has been mildly cured, soaking will not be necessary.
2. Place the corned beef in a 5- or 6-quart pot and cover it with enough cold water to rise at least 2 inches above the top of the meat.
3. Bring to a boil, skimming off any scum that rises to the surface.
4. Half cover the pot, turn the heat to its lowest point (the liquid should barely simmer) and cook the beef from 3 to 4 hours, or until tender. If necessary, add more hot water to the pot from time to time to keep the meat constantly covered.
5. Cook the cabbage separately in boiling salted water for about 15 minutes.
6. The potatoes, carrots and onions may be cooked together in their own pot of salted boiling water.
7. The beets, however, require different treatment. Scrub them thoroughly, then cut off their tops, leaving 1 inch of stem.
8. Cover them with boiling water and bring to a boil.
9. Simmer the beets from ½ to 1½ hours,

or until they are tender. Let them cool a bit, then slip off their skins.

10. To serve the dinner in the traditional way, slice the corned beef and arrange it along the center of a large heated platter.

11. Surround the meat with the vegetables and sprinkle the vegetables with chopped parsley.

12. Horseradish, mustard and a variety of pickles make excellent accompaniments to this hearty meal.

Boiled Beef with Chive Sauce

Rindfleisch mit Schmittlauchsosse   *To serve 4 to 6*

3 pounds lean boneless beef chuck or lean brisket of beef
2 medium-sized carrots, scraped
2 celery stalks, with their leaves
1 leek, white part only
1 large onion, peeled
4 parsley sprigs
5 whole black peppercorns
2 teaspoons salt
4 tablespoons butter
3 tablespoons flour

½ cup light cream
¼ cup finely chopped fresh chives, or substitute ¼ cup green scallion tops, finely chopped
¼ teaspoon ground nutmeg

1. Place the beef in a heavy 4- to 5-quart heatproof casserole or Dutch oven, and pour in enough water to cover the beef by about 2 inches.

2. Bring to a boil over high heat, meanwhile skimming off any scum that rises to the surface.

3. Add the carrots, celery stalks, leek, onion, parsley sprigs, peppercorns and salt, then reduce the heat to its lowest point, partially cover the casserole, and simmer for 2½ to 3 hours, or until the meat shows no resistance when pierced with a fork.

4. Transfer the meat to a heated plate and cover it with aluminum foil to keep it warm.

5. Strain the cooking stock into a bowl and discard the vegetables.

6. Skim as much of the surface fat from the stock as you can.

7. In a heavy 8- to 10-inch skillet, melt the butter over moderate heat, and when the foam subsides, add the flour.

8. Stirring constantly, cook the mixture for 1 or 2 minutes. Do not let the flour brown.

9. Slowly pour in 2 cups of the strained stock and then the cream. Bring the sauce to a boil, beating constantly with a whisk until it is thick and smooth.

10. Reduce the heat to low and simmer for 10 minutes.

11. Add the chives and nutmeg and taste for seasoning.

12. If the sauce is too thick for your taste, thin with a few tablespoons of the reserved stock.

13. To serve, carve the meat into thin slices and arrange them slightly overlapping on a large, heated platter.

14. Spoon a few tablespoons of the sauce over the meat and pass the rest separately in a sauceboat.

Boiled beef shown with browned potatoes, is a wholesome Austrian specialty usually served with a creamy horseradish sauce.

Austrian Boiled Beef

Gekochtes Rindfleisch   *To serve 4 to 6*

A 3-pound boneless beef rump, bottom
  round, brisket or chuck roast, tied
3 pounds chicken parts (back, wings,
  giblets, necks)
2 quarts water
1 teaspoon salt
3 tablespoons butter
2 cups onions, quartered
1 parsnip, scraped and cut into 1-inch
  chunks
3 carrots, cut into 1-inch chunks
4 large celery ribs, cut into 2-inch pieces
1 leek, white part only
4 sprigs parsley
1 bay leaf
6 peppercorns
4 whole allspice

1. In a 6- or 8-quart saucepan or soup ket-tle, combine the beef and chicken parts and cover them with the water. Add the salt.
2. Bring to a boil over high heat, adding more water, if necessary, to cover. Skim off sur-face scum as it rises.
3. Meanwhile, in a heavy 12-inch skillet, heat the butter.
4. When the foam subsides, add the onions, parsnip, carrots, celery, leek and parsley.
5. Over high heat, toss the vegetables in the hot butter for 4 or 5 minutes, or until they are lightly browned. Scrape them in the soup kettle and bring the liquid to a boil again, skim off the surface scum and add the bay leaf,

peppercorns and allspice.
6. Turn the heat to its lowest point, partially cover the pot and simmer for about 2 hours, or until the beef shows no resistance when pierced with the point of a sharp knife.
7. Remove the beef to a heated serving platter.
8. Then skim the surface fat from the stock and strain the stock through a large sieve, pressing down hard on the vegetables before discarding them. Taste for seasoning. The stock may be served as a soup.

HORSERADISH SAUCE
¼ cup bottled horseradish, drained and
  squeezed dry in a kitchen towel
1 tablespoon white wine vinegar
1 teaspoon sugar
¼ teaspoon dry English mustard
½ teaspoon salt
½ teaspoon white pepper
½ cup chilled heavy cream

1. In a small bowl, stir the horseradish, vinegar, sugar, mustard, salt and white pep-per together until well blended.
2. Beat the cream with a whisk or a rotary or electric beater until stiff enough to form un-wavering peaks on the beater when it is lifted from the bowl.
3. Pour the horseradish mixture over the cream and, with a spatula, fold together lightly but thoroughly. Taste for seasoning.
4. Serve the sauce from a sauceboat as an accompaniment to the beef.

Boiled Beef
with Dumplings

To serve 6

MEAT

A 3- to 3½-pound lean corned beef brisket, rolled and tied

18 peeled white onions, about 1 inch in diameter (about 1 pound)

12 small scraped carrots

1. Place the brisket in a 5- to 6-quart casserole, and add enough water to cover it by at least ½ inch.

2. Bring to a boil over high heat, meanwhile skimming off the scum and foam as they rise to the surface. Reduce the heat, partially cover the casserole, and simmer for 2½ hours.

3. Then add the onions and carrots, and cook partially covered for another 30 minutes, or until the vegetables are tender and the meat shows no resistance when pierced with a fork.

DUMPLINGS

1 cup all-purpose flour

½ teaspoon double-acting baking powder

½ teaspoon salt

1½ ounces fresh beef suet, finely chopped and thoroughly chilled (about 3 tablespoons)

⅓ cup milk

1. Meanwhile, preheat the oven to 250° and make the dumpling mixture.

2. Sift the flour, baking powder and salt into a large bowl. Add the suet and, working quickly, rub the flour and fat together with your fingertips until the mixture looks like flakes of coarse meal.

3. Pour the milk over the mixture, toss together lightly, and gather the dough into a ball. If the dough crumbles, add up to 2 more tablespoons of milk, a drop or two at a time, until the particles adhere.

4. With lightly floured hands, shape the dough into 1-inch balls.

5. With a slotted spoon, remove the meat and vegetables from the hot stock, and arrange them on a large heated platter. Cover and keep them warm in the oven.

6. Drop the dumplings into the hot stock remaining in the casserole, stirring gently once or twice.

7. Cook uncovered over moderate heat for 15 minutes, or until the dumplings rise to the surface.

8. Transfer the dumplings to the platter of beef and vegetables, and serve at once, accompanied if you like by horseradish sauce (page 25).

Rolled Steak with Onions

Sobrebarriga   *To serve 4*

A 2-pound flank steak, trimmed of all fat
1½ teaspoons salt
Freshly ground black pepper
3 tablespoons olive oil
1 cup coarsely chopped onions
½ cup finely diced celery
½ teaspoon finely chopped garlic
5 cups water
1 teaspoon ground cumin seeds

1. Preheat the oven to 350°.

2. Season both sides of the steak with 1 teaspoon of the salt and a few grindings of pepper.

3. Then roll the steak with the grain in jelly-roll fashion, and tie it at both ends and in the middle with kitchen cord.

4. In a heavy 3- to 4-quart heatproof casserole, heat 2 tablespoons of the oil over high heat until a light haze forms above it.

5. Add the rolled steak and brown it on all sides. Regulate the heat so that the steak browns quickly without burning.

6. Transfer the steak to a plate and, to the fat remaining in the casserole, add ½ cup of the onions, the celery and garlic.

7. Cook over moderate heat, stirring frequently, for 5 minutes, or until the vegetables are soft but not brown.

8. Return the steak and any juice on the plate to the casserole, pour in the water and bring to a boil over high heat.

9. Cover the casserole, place it in the oven and cook for 2 hours, or until the steak shows no resistance when pierced with the tip of a knife.

10. Remove the casserole from the oven and increase the heat to 400°.

11. In a 6- to 8-inch skillet, heat the remaining tablespoon of oil over moderate heat and add the remaining ½ cup of onions.

12. Stir in the cumin and ½ teaspoon of salt and cook for 3 minutes.

13. Spread the remaining onions on top of the steak.

14. Return the casserole to the oven and bake, uncovered, for 15 minutes, or until the onions are lightly browned.

15. Slice the steak into ¼-inch rounds and arrange them attractively on a heated platter.

16. Pour the pan juices over them and serve immediately.

Stuffed Beef Roll

Farsu Magru   *To serve 6 to 8*

1 whole egg
2 egg yolks
2 slices French or Italian bread, torn into tiny pieces
¼ pound lean veal, ground twice
2 tablespoons freshly grated imported Parmesan cheese
1 tablespoon finely chopped parsley
½ teaspoon salt
Freshly ground black pepper
A three-pound slice of round steak, cut 1 inch thick, trimmed, butterflied (slit horizontally almost all the way through and opened out flat), and pounded ¼ inch thick
¼ pound Italian salami, cut into 1-by-¼-inch julienne strips
2 ounces *provolone* cheese, cut into 1-by-¼-inch julienne strips
2 hard-cooked eggs, quartered
¼ cup olive oil
½ cup finely chopped onions
1 teaspoon finely chopped garlic
1 cup dry red wine
1 bay leaf
4 cups canned Italian plum or whole-pack tomatoes, chopped but not drained (a 2-pound 3-ounce can)
2 tablespoons tomato paste

1. In a large mixing bowl, stir the egg, egg yolks and pieces of bread together until they are well mixed.

2. With a spoon beat in the ground veal, grated cheese, parsley, salt and a few gridings of pepper.

3. Spread the pounded round steak out flat on a table. With a small metal spatula or knife, spread the stuffing mixture evenly over the steak.

4. Arrange the julienne strips of salami and *provolone* and the quartered eggs on the stuffing, pressing them lightly into place.

5. Starting from one long edge of the steak,

carefully roll it up like a jelly roll. It will look like a long salami.

6. With short lengths of string, tie the roll together crosswise in at least 5 or 6 places to keep it in shape.

7. Preheat the oven to 325°.

8. To cook the beef roll, you will need a heavy heatproof casserole or baking pan that has a cover and is large enough to hold the beef roll comfortably.

9. Pour in the olive oil and heat it until a light haze forms over it.

10. Brown the beef roll in the hot oil, turning it with 2 spoons until it is richly colored on all sides.

11. Remove the beef and set it aside on a plate.

12. Discard almost all of the fat from the casserole, leaving just a thin film on the bottom. Add the onions and garlic and cook them over moderate heat, stirring frequently, for 8 to 10 minutes, or until they are soft and lightly colored.

13. Pour in the wine and boil it briskly over high heat to reduce it to ½ cup, stirring constantly and scraping in any browned fragments that cling to the casserole.

14. Return the beef roll to the casserole and add the bay leaf.

15. Force the tomatoes and tomato paste through a sieve of food mill directly into the casserole. With this addition, the liquid should now come about ⅔ of the way up the side of the roll; add more beef broth or water if necessary.

16. Bring to a boil over high heat, drape a strip of aluminum foil over the beef roll and cover the casserole.

17. Cook on the middle shelf of the oven for about 1½ hours, or until the meat is tender when pierced with the tip of a sharp knife.

18. Transfer the beef roll to a carving board and strain the sauce from the casserole through a sieve or food mill into a small saucepan. Skim off most of its fat, then boil

the sauce over high heat, stirring constantly, until it is thick enough to coat a spoon heavily.

19. Cut the strings from the beef, carve the roll into 1-inch slices and arrange these attractively on a heated platter.

20. Spoon the sauce over and around the beef.

Beef Birds with Pea Purée

To serve 4

BEEF BIRDS
8 thin slices round of beef
6 chicken livers
3 tablespoons butter
¼ pound mushrooms, sliced
Salt
Pepper
8 thin slices cooked ham or tongue
3 tablespoons brandy
1 teaspoon meat glaze
½ teaspoon tomato paste
2 teaspoons potato flour
1¼ cups beef stock
¼ cup red wine
1 bay leaf

1. Put the slices of beef between 2 pieces of wax paper and beat until very thin with a wooden mallet.
2. Brown 6 chicken livers quickly in 1 tablespoon of melted butter. Remove them from the pan.
3. Put another tablespoon of butter into the pan and sauté ¼ pound sliced mushrooms until lightly browned.
4. Shred the chicken livers and mix with the mushrooms, salt and pepper.
5. Put a thin slice of ham or tongue on each piece of beef with a spoonful of the mushroom mixture on top. Press down carefully.
6. Roll each slice of beef and bind each end with string.
7. Brown these beef birds quickly all over in 1 tablespoon of melted butter.
8. Heat 3 tablespoons of brandy in a small pan, ignite and pour over the beef birds. Remove them from the pan.
9. Blend in, off the fire, 1 teaspoon of meat glaze, ½ teaspoon of tomato paste and 2 teaspoons of potato flour.
10. Pour on 1¼ cups of stock and ¼ cup of red wine and stir over the fire until the mixture comes to a boil. Taste for seasoning.
11. Put back the beef birds with a bay leaf. Cover and cook gently until the beef is tender, about 45 minutes.
12. While the beef is simmering, prepare a pea purée.

PEA PUREE
3 cups fresh or frozen peas
Salt
2 tablespoons butter
2 tablespoons flour
Pepper
3 tablespoons sour cream

1. Cook 3 cups of shelled fresh or frozen peas in boiling salted water until very tender. Drain well and put through a strainer.
2. Melt 2 tablespoons of butter in a small pan.
3. Stir in 2 tablespoons of flour, salt and pepper, and brown very slowly.
4. Add the strained peas, 3 tablespoons of sour cream and a little more seasoning. Keep warm in a double boiler until ready for use.

TO SERVE: 1. Make a bed of pea purée on a hot serving dish.
2. Remove the beef birds, cut off the strings and arrange the beef birds on top of the pea purée.
3. Strain the sauce over all.

Rich brown rolls of beef are made of top-round-steak slices seasoned with hot prepared mustard and stuffed with dill pickles, bacon and chopped onions.

Braised Stuffed Beef Rolls

Rouladen   *To serve 6*

3 pounds top round steak, sliced ½ inch thick, trimmed of all fat and pounded ¼ inch thick
6 teaspoons Düsseldorf-style prepared mustard, or substitute 6 teaspoons other hot prepared mustard
¼ cup finely chopped onions
6 slices lean bacon, each about 8 inches long
3 dill pickles, rinsed in cold water and cut lengthwise into halves
3 tablespoons lard
2 cups water
1 cup coarsely chopped celery
¼ cup thinly sliced leeks, white part only
1 tablespoon finely chopped scraped parsnip
3 parsley sprigs
1 teaspoon salt
1 tablespoon butter
2 tablespoons flour

1. Cut the steak into 6 rectangular pieces about 4 inches wide and 8 inches long.
2. Spread each rectangle with a teaspoon of mustard, sprinkle it with 2 teaspoons of onions, and place a slice of bacon down the center.
3. Lay a strip of pickle across the narrow end of each piece and roll the meat around it, jelly-roll fashion, into a cylinder. Tie the rolls at each end with kitchen cord.
4. In a heavy 10- to 12-inch skillet melt the lard over moderate heat until it begins to splutter.
5. Add the beef rolls, and brown them on all sides, regulating the heat so they color quickly and evenly without burning.
6. Transfer the rolls to a plate, pour the water into the skillet and bring it to a boil, meanwhile scraping in any brown particles clinging to the bottom and sides of the pan.
7. Add the celery, leeks, parsnip, parsley and salt, and return the beef rolls to the skillet.
8. Cover, reduce the heat to low, and simmer for 1 hour, or until the meat shows no resistance when pierced with a fork. Turn the rolls once or twice during the cooking period.
9. Transfer the rolls to a heated platter, and cover with foil to keep them warm while you make the sauce.
10. Strain the cooking liquid left in the skillet through a fine sieve, pressing down hard on the vegetables before discarding them. Measure the liquid, return it to the skillet, and boil briskly until it is reduced to 2 cups. Remove from the heat.
11. Melt the butter in a small saucepan over moderate heat and, when the foam subsides, sprinkle in the flour.
12. Lower the heat and cook, stirring constantly, until the flour turns a golden brown. Be careful not to let it burn.
13. Gradually add the reduced cooking liquid, beating vigorously with a whisk until the sauce is smooth and thick.
14. Taste for seasoning and return the sauce and the *Rouladen* to the skillet.
15. Simmer over low heat only long enough to heat the rolls through.
16. Serve the rolls on a heated platter and pour the sauce over them. *Rouladen* are often accompanied by red cabbage and dumplings or boiled potatoes.

Matambre, an Argentine beef roll, dates from stagecoach days
when travelers took them along to eat while crossing the Pampa.

Stuffed Flank-Steak Roll

Matambre   *To serve 8 to 10*

2 two-pound flank steaks
½ cup red wine vinegar
1 teaspoon finely chopped garlic
1 teaspoon dried thyme

THE STUFFING
½ pound fresh spinach
8 scraped cooked whole carrots, about 6 to
8 inches long and no more than 1 inch in diameter
4 hard-cooked eggs, cut lengthwise into quarters
1 large onion, sliced ⅛ inch thick and divided into rings
¼ cup finely chopped fresh parsley
1 teaspoon crumbled *pequín* chili
1 tablespoon coarse salt
3 cups beef stock, fresh or canned
1 to 3 cups cold water

A Sharp Knife and Sure Touch to Butterfly Steaks

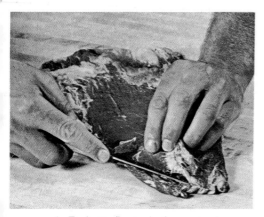

1. To butterfly steaks for *matambre*, slice into each one horizontally from one side, using your sharpest knife.

2. Continuing to slice horizontally, slit the steak almost in half, cutting to within ½ inch of the far side.

3. Open the steak out flat when you finish the cutting – its shape will be similar to that of a butterfly.

Filling, Rolling and Tying the Steaks

4. After marinating the butterflied steaks, place them end to end, overlapping them by about 2 inches.

5. Spread both steaks with the *matambre* stuffing: spinach leaves, carrots, hard-cooked eggs, onion rings, parsley, chili and salt. Then, beginning at either of the short ends, roll the steaks with the grain, jelly-roll fashion.

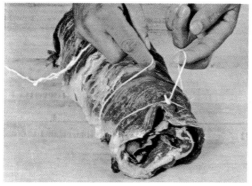

6. Roll the steaks together carefully and as compactly as possible until they form a long, thick cylinder.

7. Tie the rolled steaks with one long cord, looping it at 1-inch intervals (*see recipe, page 34*).

8. Cook the *matambre* in a heavy casserole or roasting pan just large enough to hold it snugly.

1. Ask your butcher to butterfly the steaks, or do it yourself in the following fashion: With a long sharp knife slit the steaks horizontally from one long side to within ½ inch of the other side.

2. Open the steaks, place them between 2 sheets of wax paper, and pound them with the side of a cleaver to flatten them further. Trim away all gristle and fat.

3. Lay one steak, cut side up, on a 12-by-18-inch jelly-roll pan. Sprinkle it with half the vinegar, then scatter half the garlic and thyme over it.

4. Cover the meat with the other steak, also cut side up, and sprinkle it with the remaining vinegar, garlic and thyme.

5. Cover the pan and let the steaks marinate for 6 hours at room temperature or overnight refrigerated.

6. Preheat the oven to 375°.

7. Lay the steaks end to end, cut side up, so that they overlap by about 2 inches.

8. Pound the joined ends together with the flat of a cleaver to seal them securely.

9. Wash the spinach under running water, drain it and trim off the stems.

10. Spread the leaves evenly over the meat, and arrange the carrots across the grain of the meat in parallel rows about 3 inches apart.

11. Place the eggs between the rows of carrots. Scatter the onion rings over them and sprinkle the surface evenly with parsley, chili and salt.

12. Carefully roll the steaks with the grain, jelly-roll fashion, into a thick, long cylinder.

13. To tie the *matambre,* cut a kitchen cord into a 10-foot length. Wrap one end of the cord around the steaks about 1 inch from the edge of the roll and knot it securely. Then, holding the cord in a loop near the knot, wrap the remaining length of cord around the steaks about 2 inches from the edge of the roll and feed it through the loop. Now tighten

the cord to keep the loop in place.

14. Repeat until the roll is tied in loops at intervals of about 1 inch. Bring the remaining cord across the length of the bottom of the roll (catching it in one or two loops) and up over the opposite end. Tie it securely around the first loop. Trim off any excess cord.

15. Place the *matambre* in a 12-quart casserole or roasting pan and pour in the stock. Add enough cold water to come a third of the way up the roll.

16. Then cover tightly and place in the middle of the oven for 1 hour.

17. To serve hot, remove the *matambre* from the pan to a board and let it rest for 10 minutes.

18. With a sharp knife remove the strings and cut the *matambre* into ¼-inch slices.

19. Arrange the slices on a heated platter and moisten them with a little pan liquid before serving.

20. Or the *matambre* may be thoroughly chilled, and served in similarly cut slices.

21. In Argentina, the *matambre* is generally poached in stock or water to cover it completely; it is then removed from the pot, pressed under weights until the juices drain off, refrigerated and served cold.

Planked Steak

To serve 4

A 2½- to 3-pound porterhouse steak
1 clove garlic, crushed
7 tablespoons butter
Salt
Pepper
4 tomatoes
8 large mushrooms
1 cup finely chopped onion
4 sautéed chicken livers, chopped
½ pound cooked ham, ground
1 teaspoon chopped parsley
3 tablespoons sour cream
2 tablespoons grated Parmesan cheese
6 medium-sized old potatoes
2 eggs
½ cup hot milk

1. Rub the steak with 1 clove of crushed garlic, brush with 2 tablespoons of melted butter and season with salt and pepper.
2. Broil on one side only. Place the steak, uncooked side up, on a large wooden plank that has been rubbed with oil.
3. Prepare the following stuffing for the tomatoes and mushroom caps.
4. Chop the mushroom stems and sauté in 1 tablespoon of butter with 1 cup of finely chopped onion until soft and lightly browned.
5. Blend with 4 sautéed chopped chicken livers, ½ pound of ground cooked ham, 1 teaspoon of chopped parsley, 3 tablespoons of sour cream, salt and pepper.
6. Cut the tops off 4 tomatoes and scoop out the seedy pulp with a spoon.
7. Fill with the stuffing, top with 2 tablespoons of grated Parmesan cheese and 2 tablespoons of melted butter.
8. Fill 4 mushroom caps with the same mixture, cover with the other 4 caps and sprinkle with the remaining melted butter.
9. Peel 6 potatoes and cook for about 20 minutes in boiling salted water, or until tender.
10. Drain and dry for a minute or so over a slow fire.
11. Put through a ricer or strainer, beat in 1 egg, ½ cup of hot creamy milk, salt and pepper.
12. Place the mushrooms and tomatoes alternately around the steak.
13. Pipe the potatoes all around the edge, using a pastry bag with a large rose tube.
14. Brush the potatoes with a slightly beaten egg.
15. Place under the broiler, 3 to 4 inches away from the flame, for 8 to 10 minutes.
16. Serve on the plank.

NOTE: Four *filets mignons* may be used instead of porterhouse steak to simplify carving. Or the steak may be boned before it is cooked.

Steaks Eszterházy are portions of top-round steak served with a rich, piquant sauce and garnished with strips of parsnips, carrots and gherkin pickles.

11/18/86

Steaks Eszterházy

Eszterházy Rostélyos   *To serve 6*

Salt
Freshly ground black pepper
2 pounds top round steak ½ inch thick,
   cut into 6 equal portions
Flour
3 tablespoons lard
1½ cups finely chopped onions
½ teaspoon finely chopped garlic
½ cup finely chopped carrots
3 tablespoons beef stock, fresh or canned
3 whole allspice or ⅛ teaspoon ground
   allspice
3 medium-sized bay leaves
4 peppercorns
⅛ teaspoon thyme
⅛-inch-wide strip lemon peel
4 slices lean bacon, coarsely chopped (⅓
   cup)
2 tablespoons finely chopped parsley
¼ cup white wine vinegar
¾ cup heavy cream
1 teaspoon fresh lemon juice
THE GARNISH
2 parsnips, scraped and cut into
   3-by-½-inch julienne strips
1 medium-sized carrot, cut into
   3-by-½-inch julienne strips
4 sour gherkin pickles, cut into
   3-by-½-inch julienne strips

1. Salt and pepper the steaks, then dip them in flour and shake them to remove the excess.
2. Heat the lard in a 12-inch skillet until a light haze forms over it, then brown the steaks over high heat for about 3 minutes on each side.
3. Remove them to a platter and reduce the heat to medium.
4. Add the onions, garlic and carrots and cook for about 8 minutes, stirring frequently, until the vegetables are lightly colored.
5. Off the heat, stir in 3 tablespoons of flour, continuing to stir until all the flour is absorbed.
6. Return the skillet to the heat, add the stock and bring it to a boil, stirring constantly with a whisk until the sauce is smooth and thick.
7. Add the allspice, bay leaves, peppercorns, thyme, lemon peel, bacon, parsley and vinegar.
8. Return the meat to the skillet and bring the stock to a boil again.
9. Reduce the heat to low, partially cover the pan and simmer for 50 minutes to an hour, or until the steaks show no resistance when pierced with the tip of a small sharp knife.
10. Drop the parsnip and carrot strips into a saucepan of boiling, lightly salted water.
11. Boil uncovered for 2 or 3 minutes, or until the vegetables are slightly tender, then drain in a colander or sieve.
12. Arrange the steaks on a platter and keep them warm in a 200° oven while you prepare the sauce.
13. Strain the contents of the frying pan, pressing hard on the vegetables before discarding them.
14. Skim off the surface fat from the sauce.
15. Whisk the cream and lemon juice into the sauce and add the carrot, parsnip and gherkin strips.
16. Simmer 2 or 3 minutes. Taste for seasoning.
17. Pour the vegetables and the sauce over the steaks and serve at once.

Swedish Roulades

Pikanta Oxrulader To serve 4

2 pounds top round steak
4 tablespoons butter
4 tablespoons vegetable oil
1 cup finely chopped onions
2 tablespoons flour
Salt
Freshly ground black pepper
16 flat anchovy fillets, washed and dried
½ cup water

1. Ask the butcher to cut the meat in 8 slices of 6 by 3 inches each and to pound them to ⅛ inch thick, or pound them yourself between 2 pieces of wax paper with a meat pounder or the flat of a cleaver. Trim to the above size.
2. Heat 1 tablespoon of the butter with 2 tablespoons of the oil in a small skillet and in it sauté the chopped onions for 5 to 8 minutes, or until they are tender and golden.
3. Remove from the heat and stir in the flour.
4. Now return to low heat and cook for 1 or 2 minutes, stirring constantly.
5. Reserve 2 tablespoons of this *roux* for the sauce.
6. Sprinkle each slice of meat liberally with salt and a few grindings of pepper, and spread the remainder of the *roux* evenly over the meat.
7. Lay 2 anchovy fillets on each slice, roll them up securely and either tie with a loop of cord at each end or fasten with a wooden toothpick inserted through the roll lengthwise.
8. Heat the remaining 3 tablespoons of butter and 2 tablespoons of oil in a heavy 10- to 12-inch sauté pan over moderate heat. When the foam subsides, add the roulades, 4 at a time.
9. Turn the roulades with kitchen tongs to brown them on all sides.
10. Arrange the browned roulades in a single layer in a 2- to 2½-quart casserole or baking dish that is equipped with a cover. The

preparation of the roulades may be done in advance up to this point.
11. Preheat the oven to 350°.
12. Deglaze the pan by pouring in the ½ cup of water and boiling for 1 or 2 minutes, stirring to scrape up any bits clinging to the pan.
13. Add 2 tablespoons of the *roux* that you have kept aside and cook over medium-high heat for 2 or 3 minutes, still stirring briskly, until the sauce has thickened.
14. Pour over the roulades, cover and bake for 45 minutes.

11/84

Steak with Sour-Cream Sauce

Zwiebelfleisch To serve 4 to 6

2 tablespoons vegetable oil
2 tablespoons butter
2 pounds beef tenderloin or other tender cut of beefsteak, cut into strips 2 inches long, 1 inch wide and ¼ inch thick
1¼ cups finely chopped onions
½ teaspoon finely chopped garlic
½ teaspoon caraway seeds
⅛ teaspoon marjoram
Freshly ground black pepper
2 tablespoons white vinegar
1 cup beef stock, fresh or canned

1. In a heavy 10- or 12-inch skillet, heat the oil and butter. When the foam subsides, add the meat and brown it on both sides – about 5 minutes in all.
2. Remove it to a platter.
3. Pour off most of the fat, leaving only a thin film on the bottom of the skillet.
4. Add the onions and cook them, stirring

occasionally, for 8 to 10 minutes, or until they are lightly colored, then add the garlic and cook for about 3 minutes longer.

5. Stir in the caraway seeds, the marjoram and a generous grinding of pepper. Add the vinegar and boil for 1 minute.

6. Pour in the stock and bring to a boil, stirring in any brown bits that cling to the bottom and sides of the pan.

7. Return the meat to the pan and bring the beef stock to a boil again.

8. Turn the heat to low and simmer the meat for 15 minutes or longer until it is tender.

THE SAUCE
1 tablespoon flour
1 cup sour cream

1. In the meanwhile with a wire whisk, beat the flour into the sour cream in a small mixing bowl.

2. With a large spoon stir the mixture into the skillet, then turn the heat to its lowest point and simmer for 10 minutes without letting the sauce reach the boiling point.

3. Mask the steak with some of the sauce and serve the rest in a sauceboat.

Portuguese Steak

Bife à Portuguêsa   *To serve 4*

4 large peeled garlic cloves, 2 crushed with a cleaver or knife and cut 2 lengthwise into halves
1 tablespoon red wine vinegar
1 tablespoon salt
Freshly ground black pepper
4 beef tenderloin steaks, sliced about ¾ inch thick
2 tablespoons olive oil

2 tablespoons butter
1 large bay leaf, crumbled
8 thin slices *presunto* ham or prosciutto or other lean smoked ham
¼ cup dry red wine
1 teaspoon fresh lemon juice
2 teaspoons finely chopped parsley
1 lemon cut into 8 wedges

1. Preheat the oven to 250°.

2. Mash the crushed garlic, vinegar, salt and a few grindings of pepper to a smooth paste with a mortar and pestle or in a bowl with the back of a spoon.

3. With your fingers, rub the paste into the steaks, pressing it firmly into both sides of the meat.

4. In a heavy 10- to 12-inch skillet, melt the butter in the olive oil over moderate heat. When the foam has almost subsided, add the garlic halves and bay leaf and cook for 1 minute, stirring constantly.

5. Then, with a slotted spoon, remove and discard the garlic and bay leaf.

6. Add the steaks and cook for 2 or 3 minutes on each side, turning them with tongs, and regulating the heat so that they color quickly and evenly. The steaks should be well browned, but still pink inside.

7. Transfer the steaks to individual baking dishes or fairly deep plates and keep them warm in the oven.

8. Add the slices of ham to the fat remaining in the skillet and cook over high heat, turning them frequently for 1 or 2 minutes.

9. With the tongs, place 2 slices of ham on each steak.

10. Pour off all but a thin film of fat from the skillet, add the wine and lemon juice and bring to a boil over high heat, meanwhile scraping in any brown particles clinging to the bottom and sides of the pan.

11. Pour the sauce over the steaks, sprinkle them with parsley and garnish each serving with lemon wedges.

12. Serve at once.

Fried Steak
with Cellophane Noodles

Kan-shao-nu-jou-ssŭ   *To serve 2*

**Half of a 2-ounce package of cellophane
   noodles**
½ pound flank steak
2 tablespoons soy sauce
1 teaspoon cornstarch
½ teaspoon sugar
**2 cups peanut oil, or flavorless vegetable
   oil**
**1 green pepper, seeded, deribbed and
   shredded into strips 1½ to 2 inches long
   and ⅛ inch wide**
1 teaspoon finely chopped fresh ginger root
**¼ to ½ teaspoon cayenne pepper, accord-
   ing to taste**

PREPARE AHEAD: 1. With a sharp knife or a
pair of scissors, cut the cellophane noodles
into 4-inch lengths, separating any noodles
that cling together.
2. With a cleaver or sharp, heavy knife, trim
off and discard the fat from the flank steak.
To shred the steak, put it in the freezer for
30 minutes or so to firm the meat and make
it easier to slice. Then lay the steak flat on
a chopping board and slice the meat horizontally (with the grain) as thin as possible. Cut
these slices into pieces 1½ to 2 inches long
and ⅛ inch wide.
3. In a small bowl combine the soy sauce,
cornstarch and sugar. Add the shredded steak
and toss it about in the bowl until it is well
coated with the mixture.
4. Have the noodles, steak, oil, green pepper, ginger and cayenne pepper within easy
reach.

TO COOK: 1. Set a 12-inch wok or 10-inch
skillet over high heat and pour in the 2 cups
of oil.
2. Heat the oil until it smokes, or it registers
450° on a deep-frying thermometer.
3. Drop in half of the noodles and let them

deep-fry for one second. As soon as they puff
up, lift them out with a slotted spoon and
spread them on a double thickness of paper
towels to drain.
4. Then fry the other half of the noodles.
5. Pour off the oil and set it aside in a small
mixing bowl.
6. Return the wok or skillet to the heat and
return 1 tablespoon of the oil to the pan. Swirl
it about in the pan and let it heat for 30
seconds, turning the heat down to moderate
if the oil begins to smoke.
7. Drop in the green pepper and stir-fry for
2 minutes until it begins to darken in color.
8. With a slotted spoon, transfer the green
pepper to a plate.
9. Add another 2 tablespoons of oil to the
pan and let it heat for 30 seconds.
10. Add the ginger root, and stir it about for
1 or 2 seconds, then add the shredded flank
steak and cayenne pepper, and stir-fry for 1
to 2 minutes, until the beef is lightly browned
and any liquid which may have accumulated
in the pan has completely evaporated.
11. Return the green pepper to the pan and
heat it through, stirring constantly.
12. To serve, place the beef and pepper mixture in the center of a large heated platter and
arrange the fried cellophane noodles around
the outside.

Viennese Steaks

Wiener Rostbraten   *To serve 6*

**6 medium-sized onions, peeled and thinly
   sliced**
4 tablespoons butter
**3 pounds boneless beef sirloin cut ½ inch
   thick, then pounded to ¼ inch thick**
3 tablespoons vegetable oil
2 tablespoons butter
Salt
Freshly ground black pepper
½ cup beef stock, fresh or caned (optional)

1. Cut the sliced onions into strips ⅛ to ¼ inch wide.

2. In a heavy 8- or 10-inch skillet over medium heat, melt the 4 tablespoons of butter, and when the foam subsides, add the onions.

3. Stirring occasionally, cook them for 8 to 10 minutes, or until they are colored and crisp. Add more butter if necessary while the onions are frying – they must not burn.

4. Set the onions aside, uncovered in the skillet.

5. Cut the steak into 6 equal portions.

6. In a 10- or 12-inch heavy skillet, heat the oil and 2 tablespoons of butter over medium heat. When the butter foam subsides, add the steaks.

7. Raise the heat to moderately high and cook the steaks briskly for 2 to 4 minutes, depending upon the degree of doneness you prefer.

8. Arrange the steaks on a heated platter and sprinkle them with salt and a few grindings of pepper.

9. Reheat the onions over high heat for a minute or so to restore their crispness.

10. Serve the steaks with a mound of the onions placed on each one.

11. If you prefer a light sauce, add the stock to the skillet in which the steaks were cooked, and bring it to a boil, stirring in any brown bits clinging to the pan, then pour the sauce over the steaks before you place the onions on top.

12. *Wiener Rostbraten* may be served with chopped parsley and crumbled bacon sprinkled over the onions.

Pepper Steak

Ching-chiao-ch'ao-niu-jou　　　　　To serve 2 to 4

1 pound flank steak, trimmed of all fat
1 tablespoon Chinese rice wine, or pale dry sherry

3 tablespoons soy sauce
1 teaspoon sugar
2 teaspoons cornstarch
2 medium-sized green peppers, seeded, deribbed and cut into ½-inch squares
4 slices peeled fresh ginger root, about 1 inch in diameter and ⅛ inch thick
¼ cup peanut oil, or flavorless vegetable oil

PREPARE AHEAD: 1. Place the flank steak in your freezer for about 30 minutes, or only long enough to stiffen it slightly for easier slicing.

2. With a cleaver or sharp knife, cut the flank steak lengthwise into strips 1½ inches wide, then crosswise into ¼-inch slices.

3. In a large bowl, mix the wine, soy sauce, sugar and cornstarch. Add the steak slices and toss with a large spoon to coat them thoroughly. The steak may be cooked at once, or marinated for as long as 6 hours.

4. Place the peppers, ginger root and oil within easy reach.

TO COOK: 1. Set a 12-inch wok or 10-inch skillet over high heat for about 30 seconds.

2. Pour in a tablespoon of the oil, swirl it about in the pan and heat for another 30 seconds, turning the heat down to moderate if the oil begins to smoke.

3. Immediately add the pepper squares and stir-fry for 3 minutes, or until they are tender but still crisp.

4. Scoop them out with a slotted spoon and reserve.

5. Pour 3 more tablespoons of oil into the pan and heat almost to the smoking point.

6. Add the ginger, stir for a few seconds, then drop in the steak mixture.

7. Stir-fry over high heat for about 2 minutes, or until the meat shows no sign of pink. Discard the ginger.

8. Add the pepper and cook for a minute, stirring, then transfer the contents of the pan to a heated platter and serve.

Short Ribs with Lemon Sauce

Westfälischer Pfefferpotthast   To serve 4

2 pounds beef short ribs, cut into 2-inch
  pieces
Salt
Freshly ground black pepper
2 tablespoons lard
6 medium-sized onions (about 2 pounds),
  sliced ⅛ inch thick
1 small bay leaf
¼ teaspoon ground cloves
4 cups cold water
3 tablespoons fresh rye bread crumbs,
  made in a blender from 1 slice fresh dark
  rye bread
2 teaspoons capers, drained and rinsed in
  cold water
2 tablespoons fresh lemon juice
½ teaspoon finely grated fresh lemon peel

1. Sprinkle the short ribs with salt and pepper.
2. In a 3- to 4-quart heatproof casserole or Dutch oven, heat the lard over high heat, until it begins to splutter.
3. Add the short ribs and brown them on all sides, regulating the heat so that the ribs brown quickly and evenly without burning. Remove the meat to a platter.
4. Add the onions to the fat remaining in the casserole, and cook, stirring occasionally, for 5 minutes, or until they are soft and transparent but not brown.
5. Add the bay leaf and cloves and pour in the water.
6. Bring to a boil over high heat, scraping in any brown bits clinging to the bottom and sides of the pan.
7. Return the ribs to the casserole, cover and reduce the heat to its lowest point.
8. Simmer for 1½ hours, or until the meat shows no resistance when pierced with the tip of a small, sharp knife.
9. Then transfer the short ribs to a deep heated platter and cover with foil to keep them warm.

10. Discard the bay leaf, and skim off the fat from the liquid remaining in the casserole.
11. Stir in the bread crumbs, capers, lemon juice and lemon peel, and bring to a boil over high heat.
12. Reduce the heat; simmer uncovered, for a minute or two.
13. Taste for seasoning. The sauce should be quite peppery; add more pepper to taste if necessary.
14. Then pour the sauce over the meat and serve at once.

Steak with Red Wine Sauce

Bifteck Marchand de Vin   To serve 6

MARCHAND DE VIN SAUCE
2 tablespoons butter
½ cup finely chopped shallots or scallions
1½ cups dry red wine
½ bay leaf
¼ teaspoon dried thyme
4 parsley sprigs
2 teaspoons meat glaze combined with 3
  tablespoons hot water
12 tablespoons soft butter (1½ quarter-
  pound sticks)
1 tablespoon lemon juice
1 tablespoon flour
2 tablespoons finely chopped fresh parsley

1. In a 1- to 2-quart enameled saucepan, melt 2 tablespoons of butter over moderate heat.
2. When the foam subsides, cook the shallots, stirring constantly, for 2 minutes, or until they are soft.
3. Pour in the wine, add the bay leaf, thyme and parsley sprigs and simmer over moderate heat until reduced to ¾ cup.
4. Strain the reduced wine through a fine sieve into a small bowl, pressing down hard on the shallots and herbs with the back of a spoon before discarding them.
5. Return the wine to the saucepan, add the thinned meat glaze and bring to a boil.

6. Set the pan aside.

7. Cream 12 tablespoons of soft butter, beating it vigorously against the side of a small bowl with a wooden spoon until it is fluffy.

8. Beat in the lemon juice, flour and parsley. Set the bowl aside.

THE STEAK

A 3- to 3½-pound sirloin, porterhouse or T-bone steak, cut 1 to 1¼ inch thick and trimmed of excess fat
1 tablespoon butter
2 tablespoons vegetable oil
Salt
Freshly ground black pepper

1. Pat the trimmed steak thoroughly dry with paper towels.

2. Cut small incisions every inch or so around the outside of the steak so it won't curl as it cooks.

3. In a heavy 12- or 14-inch skillet or sauté pan, melt 1 tablespoon of butter with the 2 tablespoons of vegetable oil over high heat.

4. Add the steak and brown it quickly for 1 or 2 minutes on each side, turning it with tongs.

5. Then reduce the heat to moderate and sauté the steak for about 5 minutes on each side, or until it is done to a medium-rare degree. Experts test a steak by pressing it with a finger. It should be slightly resilient, neither soft nor firm. If that method seems tricky, make a small incision near the bone with the tip of a sharp knife and judge by the meat's color.

6. Transfer to a heated platter and season with salt and pepper.

7. Pour the reduced wine mixture into the skillet and bring to a boil over moderate heat, stirring constantly and scraping in any browned bits from the bottom and sides of the pan.

8. Remove from the heat and blend in the creamed butter mixture, 2 tablespoons at a time.

9. To serve, slice the steak and offer the sauce separately.

Oxtail with Mustard

Queue de Boeuf Moutarde   *To serve 4*

5 tablespoons butter
3 pounds oxtail, cut up
¼ cup finely chopped onion
¼ cup soaked, chopped dried mushrooms
2 teaspoons French mustard
1 teaspoon dry mustard
3 tablespoons dry mustard
1 teaspoon meat glaze
2 teaspoons tomato paste
2 cups beef stock
Salt
Cayenne pepper
½ cup sour cream
½ cup grated Parmesan cheese
2 tablespoons chopped chives

1. Heat 2 tablespoons of butter in a deep, heavy saucepan and, when the butter is very hot, quickly brown the cut-up oxtail. Remove from the pan.

2. Put another 2 tablespoons of butter in the pan, then ¼ cup finely chopped onion and ¼ cup finely chopped dried mushrooms that have been previously soaked for an hour or so in cold water.

3. Cook very slowly for 5 to 6 minutes.

4. Blend in, off the fire, 2 teaspoons of French mustard, 1 teaspoon of dry mustard, 3 table-spoons of flour, 1 teaspoon of meat glaze and 2 teaspoons of tomato paste.

5. Pour on 2 cups of stock and stir over the fire until the mixture comes to a boil. Season with salt and cayenne pepper.

6. Put back the oxtail, cover and simmer until quite tender, about 3 to 3½ hours.

7. Remove the oxtail and arrange the pieces in a shallow, ovenproof serving dish.

8. Strain the sauce, boil it down a little, then slowly beat in ½ cup of sour cream.

9. Pour over the oxtail, sprinkle with ½ cup of grated Parmesan cheese, dot with 1 table-spoon of butter and brown under the broiler.

10. Sprinkle with chopped chives and serve at once.

Thin slices of tender beef, bamboo shoots, onions, mushrooms, Chinese chrysanthemum leaves, soybean curd, noodles and scallions are simmered at the table in soy sauce and *sake* (rice wine) to make the popular Japanese dish *sukiyaki*.

Beef with Vegetables and Soy Sauce

Sukiyaki   *To serve 4*

1 pound boneless lean beef, preferably tenderloin or sirloin
An 8-ounce can *shirataki* (long noodlelike threads), drained
1 whole canned *takenoko* (bamboo shoot)
A 2-inch-long strip of beef fat, folded into a square packet
¼ to ¾ cup Japanese all-purpose soy sauce
3 to 6 tablespoons sugar
6 scallions, including 3 inches of the stem, cut into 1½-inch pieces
1 medium-sized yellow onion, peeled and sliced ½ inch thick
4 to 6 small white mushrooms, cut into ¼-inch-thick slices
2 cakes *tofu* (soybean curd), fresh, canned or instant, cut into 1-inch cubes
2 ounces Chinese chrysanthemum leaves, watercress or Chinese cabbage
¼ to ¾ *sake* (rice wine)

PREPARE AHEAD: 1. Place the beef in your freezer for about 30 minutes, or only long enough to stiffen it slightly for easier slicing. Then, with a heavy, sharp knife, cut the beef across the grain into slices ⅛ inch thick, and cut the slices in half crosswise.
2. Bring 1 cup of water to a boil and drop in the *shirataki;* return to the boil. Drain and cut the noodles into thirds.

3. Scrape the bamboo shoot at the base, cut it in half lengthwise, and slice it thin crosswise. Run cold running water over the slices and drain.
4. Arrange the meat, *shirataki* and vegetables attractively on flat plates.

TO COOK AND SERVE: 1. If you are using an electric skillet, preheat to 425°. If not, substitute a 10- to 12-inch skillet over a table burner and preheat for several minutes.
2. Hold the folded strip of fat with chopsticks or tongs and rub it over the bottom of the hot skillet.
3. Add 6 to 8 slices of meat to the skillet, pour in ¼ cup of soy sauce, and sprinkle the meat with 3 tablespoons of sugar.
4. Cook for a minute, stir, and turn the meat over. Push the meat to one side of the skillet.
5. Add about ⅓ of the scallions, onion, mushrooms, *tofu, shirataki,* greens and bamboo shoot in more or less equal amounts, sprinkle them with ¼ cup *sake* and cook for an additional 4 to 5 minutes.
6. Transfer the contents of the pan to individual plates and serve.
7. Continue cooking the remaining *sukiyaki* batch by batch as described above, checking the temperature of the pan from time to time. If it seems too hot and the food begins to stick or burn, lower the heat or cool the pan more quickly by adding a drop or two of cold water to the sauce.

Beef *teriyaki* (page 48) is made by dipping slices of beef into a clear syrupy glaze, then broiling the slices at high heat until they are lightly browned.

Beef Strips with Onions and Peppers

Borsos Bélszíntokány   *To serve 6*

3 tablespoons lard
2½ to 3 pounds fillet of beef, cut into ¼-by-¼-by-3-inch strips
1 cup thinly sliced onions
¼ teaspoon finely chopped garlic
1 teaspoon sweet Hungarian paprika
½ cup chopped mushrooms (⅛ pound)
2 large green peppers with seeds and ribs removed, cut into strips ⅛ inch wide and 2½ inches long

1. Heat 2 tablespoons of the lard in a heavy 10-inch skillet over high heat until a light haze forms over it.
2. Add the meat strips and toss them about for 3 to 5 minutes, or until they are browned on all sides.
3. Remove the meat to a platter and add the remaining tablespoon of lard to the skillet.
4. Turn the heat to medium and add the onions and garlic.
5. Cook for 8 to 10 minutes, or until the onions are lightly colored.

6. Off the heat, stir in the paprika, continuing to stir until the onions are lightly colored.
7. Off the heat, stir in the paprika, continuing to stir until the onions are well coated.
8. Return the meat to the skillet and gently stir in the mushrooms and peppers.
9. Place the pan on high heat, and when it begins to sizzle, turn the heat to its lowest point and cover the pan tightly.
10. Simmer for 25 to 30 minutes or until the meat shows no resistance when pierced with the point of a sharp knife. Taste for seasoning.
11. Tip the skillet and skim off any of the surface fat.
12. Arrange the strips on a platter, pour the pan juices over them and serve.
13. *Borsos Bélszíntokány* is usually served with rice and sour pickles.

Braised Short Ribs

To serve 6 to 8

5 to 6 pounds lean short ribs of beef, cut into 3- to 4-inch pieces

Salt
Freshly ground black pepper
½ cup flour
2 tablespoons butter
1 cup coarsely chopped onion
1 cup coarsely chopped, scraped carrot
½ teaspoon finely chopped garlic
⅛ teaspoon thyme
1 cup beef stock, fresh or canned
2 small bay leaves

1. Preheat the oven to 500°.
2. Season the short ribs generously with salt and a few grindings of black pepper.
3. Dip them in flour, vigorously shaking off any excess, then arrange them side by side on a rack in a shallow roasting pan.
4. Brown them in the middle of the oven for 20 to 25 minutes, checking periodically to make sure they do not burn.
5. Meanwhile, melt the 2 tablespoons of butter over moderate heat in a heavy, 6-quart, heatproof casserole.
6. When the foam subsides, add the onion, carrot, garlic and thyme, and, stirring frequently, cook for 6 to 8 minutes until the vegetables are lightly colored.
7. Place the browned ribs, preferably in one layer, on top of the vegetables, add the stock to the roasting pan and stir into it any brown bits clinging to the pan. Then pour it over the ribs in the casserole.
8. Bring to a boil on top of the stove, add the bay leaves and cover the casserole tightly.
9. Reduce the oven heat to 325°.
10. Braise the short ribs in the middle of the oven for about an hour until the meat shows no resistance when pierced with a fork.
11. To serve, arrange the short ribs on a heated platter.
12. Strain the braising juices through a fine sieve into a saucepan, pressing down on the vegetables to extract all their juices before discarding them.
13. Skim the fat from the surface, taste the sauce for seasoning and pour over the meat.

Deviled Short Ribs

To serve 3 to 4

6 tablespoons butter, softened
1 tablespoon Worcestershire sauce
1 teaspoon dry English mustard
1 teaspoon curry powder (preferably imported Madras curry powder)
Freshly ground black pepper
¼ teaspoon cayenne pepper
1 teaspoon salt
2½ to 3 pounds lean short ribs of beef, each 4 to 5 inches long
½ cup flour

1. Preheat the oven to 450°.
2. With a pastry brush and 2 tablespoons of the softened butter, coat the bottom and sides of a shallow roasting pan large enough to hold the short ribs in one layer.
3. In a small bowl, cream the remaining 4 tablespoons of softened butter by beating and mashing it against the sides of the bowl with a large spoon until it is light and fluffy.
4. Then beat in the Worcestershire sauce, mustard, curry powder, 1 teaspoon of black pepper, cayenne pepper and ½ teaspoon of the salt. Set aside.
5. With a small, sharp knife, make ¼-inch-deep crisscrossing cuts about 1 inch apart on the meaty surface of the ribs.
6. Then coat them with the flour and shake them vigorously to remove any excess.
7. Sprinkle the ribs with the remaining ½ teaspoon of salt and a few grindings of pepper and arrange them fat side up in a single layer in the roasting pan.
8. Roast in the middle of the oven for 10 minutes.
9. Using a pastry brush, coat the ribs evenly with the seasoned butter, reduce the heat to 400°, and roast for 1 hour and 15 minutes, or until the meat is tender and shows no resistance when pierced with the tip of a fork.
10. Arrange the ribs on a large platter and serve at once.

Beef Slices with Sweet Glaze

Gyuniku Teriyaki   *To serve 4*

**1½ pounds lean boneless beef, preferably
   tenderloin or boneless sirloin, cut in 12
   slices ¼ inch thick**
TERIYAKI SAUCE
**1 cup *mirin* (sweet *sake*), or substitute 1
   cup less 2 tablespoons pale dry sherry**
1 cup Japanese all-purpose soy sauce
1 cup chicken stock, fresh or canned
TERIYAKI GLAZE
¼ cup *teriyaki* sauce
1 tablespoon sugar
**2 teaspoons cornstarch mixed with 1
   tablespoon cold water**
GARNISH
**4 teaspoons powdered mustard, mixed with
   just enough hot water to make a thick
   paste and set aside to rest for 15 minutes**
12 sprigs fresh parsley

PREPARE AHEAD: 1. To make the sauce, warm
the *mirin* or sherry in a 1½- to 2-quart
enameled or stainless-steel saucepan over
moderate heat. Off the heat, ignite the *mirin*
with a match, and shake the pan back and
forth until the flame dies out. Then stir in the
soy sauce and chicken stock, and bring to a
boil. Pour the sauce into a bowl and cool to
room temperature.
2. To make the glaze, combine ¼ cup of the
teriyaki sauce and 1 tablespoon of sugar in
an enameled or stainless-steel saucepan.
Bring almost to a boil over moderate heat,
then reduce the heat to low. Stir the combined cornstarch and water into the sauce.
Cook, stirring constantly, until it thickens to
a clear syrupy glaze. Immediately pour into
a dish and set aside.

TO COOK: 1. Preheat the broiler to its highest
point, or light a hibachi or charcoal grill.
2. Dip the beef, one slice at a time, into the
teriyaki sauce.
3. Broil 2 inches from the heat for 1 minute

on each side, or until lightly brown. For well-
done meat broil an additional minute.

TO SERVE: 1. Slice the meat into 1-inch-wide
strips and place them on individual serving
plates.
2. Spoon a little of the glaze over each serving, and garnish each plate with a dab of the
mustard and a sprig of parsley. If you prefer,
mix the mustard into the glaze before pouring it over the meat.

NOTE: Any leftover *teriyaki* sauce may be
stored in tightly closed jars and refrigerated
for as long as one month. Before using, bring
to a boil and skim the surface of any scum.

Beef-Stuffed Onion Rolls

Lökdolmar   *To serve 4 to 6*

½ Swedish meatball recipe (page 52)
**3 large yellow onions (½ pound each),
   peeled**
3 tablespoons butter
2 tablespoons fresh bread crumbs

1. Place the peeled onions in a 2- to 3-quart
pot, add enough cold water to cover, and
bring to a boil over moderate heat.
2. Lower the heat and simmer the onions,
uncovered, for 40 minutes.
3. Remove the onions from the pot with a

slotted spoon, drain them and let them cool on a platter while you make the meat stuffing *(recipe, page 52)*.

4. Pull off each onion layer separately. They should slide off quite easily.

5. Cut the largest outer layers of the onions in half, but remember to leave them large enough to enclose the stuffing. Discard the inner part of the onions (or use them for some other purpose) if the leaves are too small to stuff.

6. Put a heaping teaspoon of the meat stuffing in the middle of each onion leaf and enclose it by folding over the edges of the leaf.

7. Preheat the oven to 400°.

8. In a shallow 1- to 1½-quart flameproof baking dish, melt 3 tablespoons of butter over low heat.

9. Remove the dish from the heat and place the onion rolls, sealed side down, side by side in the butter, first rolling each in the butter to coat it.

10. Bake 15 minutes, then baste with the butter in the dish, sprinkle with the bread crumbs, and bake 15 minutes, or until the onions are lightly browned and the crumbs crisp.

Meatballs with Ouzo and Mint

Keftedakia   *To make 30 meatballs*

**2 slices homemade-type white bread,
    trimmed of crusts and cut or torn into
    small pieces**
**¼ cup *ouzo,* or substitute other anise-
    flavored liqueur**
7 tablespoons olive oil
½ cup finely chopped onions
1 pound lean ground beef
1 egg
**1 tablespoon finely cut fresh mint leaves,
    or substitute 1 teaspoon crumbled dried**
mint
½ teaspoon finely chopped garlic
½ teaspoon crumbled dried oregano
1 teaspoon salt
Freshly ground black pepper
1 cup flour

1. Soak the bread in the *ouzo* for at least 5 minutes.

2. Meanwhile, in a heavy 10- to 12-inch skillet, heat 3 tablespoons of the olive oil over moderate heat until a light haze forms above it.

3. Add the onions and, stirring frequently, cook for about 5 minutes, or until they are soft and transparent but not brown.

4. With a slotted spoon, transfer the onions to a large, deep mixing bowl. Set the skillet aside off the heat.

5. Squeeze the bread dry and discard the *ouzo.*

6. Add the bread, ground beef, egg, mint, garlic, oregano, salt and a few grindings of pepper to the onions.

7. Knead vigorously with both hands, then beat with a wooden spoon until the mixture is smooth and fluffy. Taste for seasoning.

8. Moistening your hands periodically with cold water, shape the beef mixture into balls about 1 inch in diameter.

9. Roll the balls in flour to coat them lightly, and refrigerate for about 1 hour.

10. Preheat the oven to 200°.

11. Add the remaining 4 tablespoons of oil to the oil in the skillet and heat over high heat until a light haze forms above it.

12. Drop 7 or 8 meatballs into the hot oil and cook them over moderate heat for 8 to 10 minutes, shaking the pan from time to time to roll the balls about and to brown them evenly.

13. Transfer the meatballs to a heatproof platter with a slotted spoon, and keep them warm in the oven while you fry the remaining balls in similar fashion. Add more oil to the pan if necessary.

Beefsteak Tartar is raw ground beef with an egg yolk. It goes well with the ingredients shown: salt, pepper, capers, onions, anchovies and parsley.

Beefsteak Tartar

To serve 2

½ **pound lean boneless beef, preferably beef tenderloin, or top or eye round, ground 2 or 3 times**
2 egg yolks
2 tablespoons salt
2 tablespoons freshly ground black pepper
2 tablespoons capers, thoroughly drained
2 tablespoons finely chopped onions
2 tablespoons finely chopped fresh parsley
8 flat anchovy fillets, thoroughly drained
Dark bread
Butter

1. Traditionally the beef for beefsteak Tartar is ground very fine and served as soon as possible thereafter.
2. Shape the beef into two mounds and place them in the center of separate serving plates.
3. Make a well in the middle of the mounds and carefully drop an egg yolk in each.
4. Serve the salt, black pepper, capers, chopped onions, parsley and anchovy fillets in small separate saucers. The beef and other ingredients are then combined to individual taste.
5. Serve with dark bread and butter.

Swedish Meatballs with Cream Sauce

Små Köttbullar   *To serve 6 to 8 (about 50 meatballs)*

1 tablespoon butter
4 tablespoons finely chopped onion
1 large boiled potato, mashed (1 cup)
3 tablespoons fine dry bread crumbs
1 pound lean ground beef
⅓ cup heavy cream
1 teaspoon salt
1 egg
**1 tablespoon finely chopped fresh parsley
  (optional)**
2 tablespoons butter
2 tablespoons vegetable oil
1 tablespoon flour
¾ cup light or heavy cream

1. In a small frying pan, melt the tablespoon of butter over moderate heat.

2. When the foam subsides, add the onions and cook for about 5 minutes, until they are soft and translucent but not brown.

3. In a large bowl, combine the onions, mashed potato, bread crumbs, meat, cream, salt, egg and optional parsley.

4. Knead vigorously with both hands or beat with a wooden spoon until all of the ingredients are well blended and the mixture is smooth and fluffy.

5. Shape into small balls about 1 inch in diameter.

6. Arrange the meatballs in one layer on a baking sheet or a flat tray, cover them with plastic wrap and chill for at least 1 hour before cooking.

7. Over high heat, melt the 2 tablespoons of butter and 2 tablespoons of oil in a heavy 10- to 12-inch skillet.

8. When the foam subsides, add the meatballs, 8 to 10 at a time.

9. Reduce the heat to moderate and fry the balls on all sides, shaking the pan almost constantly to roll the balls around in the hot fat to help keep their shape. In 8 to 10 minutes the meatballs should be brown outside and show no trace of pink inside when one is broken open with a knife.

10. Add more butter and oil to the skillet as needed, and transfer each finished batch to a casserole or baking dish and keep warm in a 200° oven.

11. To make a sauce with the pan juice, remove from the heat, pour off all of the fat from the pan, and stir in 1 tablespoon of flour. Quickly stir in ¾ cup of light or heavy cream and boil the sauce over moderate heat for 2 or 3 minutes, stirring constantly, until it is thick and smooth.

12. Pour over the meatballs and serve.

Baked Ground Beef with Okra

Bamia   *To serve 4*

1½ pounds fresh okra
**4 tablespoons butter plus 1 tablespoon
  softened butter**
½ cup finely chopped onions
1 pound ground lean beef, preferably chuck
1 teaspoon finely chopped garlic
6 tablespoons canned tomato purée
1½ to 2 cups beef stock, fresh or canned
1 teaspoon salt
Freshly ground black pepper
Lemon wedges

1. Wash the fresh okra under cold running water, and with a small, sharp knife, scrape the skin lightly to remove any surface fuzz. Cut ⅛ off the stem at the narrow end of each pod.

2. In a heavy 10- to 12-inch skillet, melt 2 tablespoons of butter over moderate heat.

3. When the foam subsides, add the okra and, stirring frequently, cook for about 5 minutes until it stops "roping," or producing thin white threads.

A sublime way to serve ground beef is the Near-Eastern dish called *bamia*, a casserole of seasoned hamburger sandwiched around spokes of fresh okra.

4. With a slotted spoon, transfer the okra to paper towels to drain.

5. Pour off the fat remaining in the skillet, add 2 more tablespoons of butter and melt it over moderate heat.

6. Drop in the onions and cook for 8 to 10 minutes, or until they are soft and lightly browned.

7. Add the meat, mashing it with the back of the spoon to break up any lumps, and cook until all traces of pink disappear.

8. Stir in the garlic, tomato purée, 1 cup of the stock, the salt and a few grindings of pepper.

9. Cook briskly uncovered until most of the liquid in the pan has evaporated and the mixture is thick enough to hold its shape almost solidly in the spoon. Remove from the heat.

10. Preheat the oven to 325°.

11. With a pastry brush coat the bottom and sides of a circular baking dish 7 or 8 inches in diameter and about 3 inches deep with the tablespoon of softened butter.

12. Spoon half the meat mixture into the casserole, smoothing and spreading it to the edges with a spatula.

13. Arrange the okra over the meat, placing the pieces closely together side by side in a spokelike pattern with the cut ends facing out.

14. Spread the remaining meat mixture evenly over the okra, masking it completely, and sprinkle over it ½ cup of the stock.

15. Bring to a boil over moderate heat, cover tightly with a lid or foil and bake in the middle of the oven for about 1 hour. (Check the casserole occasionally, and if the top seems dry pour in up to ½ cup more stock, a few tablespoons at a time.)

16. Cool the *bamia* uncovered for 5 minutes, then unmold it in the following fashion: Run a long, sharp knife around the inside edges of the casserole, place a heated serving plate upside down over the top and, grasping the casserole and plate together firmly, invert them. The *bamia* should slide out easily.

17. Serve garnished with lemon wedges.

Hamburger Mexican style is ground beef stuffed into peppers, which are then topped with cream sauce, pomegranate seeds and coriander leaves.

Chilies Stuffed with Beef

Chiles en Nogada   To serve 6

6 fresh *poblano* chilies, or substitute 6 fresh green peppers, each about 4 inches in diameter

NOTE: Wear rubber gloves when handling *poblano* chilies.

1. Roast the chilies or peppers by impaling them, one at a time, on the tines of a long-handled fork, and turning them over a gas flame until the skin blisters and darkens. Or place the chilies on a baking sheet and broil them 3 inches from the heat for about 5 minutes, turning them so that they color on all sides.

2. As the chilies are roasted, wrap them in a damp towel and let them rest for a few minutes.

3. Rub them with the towel until the skins slip off.

4. Cut out the stems and white membranes, discard the seeds.

THE FILLING
2 tablespoons lard
2 pounds ground beef, preferably chuck
1 cup coarsely chopped onions
½ teaspoon finely chopped garlic
5 medium tomatoes, peeled, seeded and

coarsely chopped, or substitute 1⅔ cups
  chopped, drained, canned Italian plum
  tomatoes
¾ cup seedless raisins
¼ cup distilled white vinegar
1½ teaspoons sugar
2 teaspoons cinnamon
½ teaspoon ground cloves
2 teaspoons salt
½ cup slivered blanched almonds

1. In a heavy 10- to 12-inch skillet, melt the lard over high heat.
2. Add the beef and brown it lightly, stirring constantly with a fork to break up any lumps.
3. Reduce the heat to moderate, add the onions and garlic, and cook 5 minutes.
4. Stir in the tomatoes, raisins, vinegar, sugar, 2 teaspoons of cinnamon, cloves and 2 teaspoons of salt; then reduce the heat and simmer, uncovered, for 15 minutes.
5. Add the slivered almonds.

THE TOPPING
2 cups heavy cream
½ cup shelled walnuts, ground in a blender
  or pulverized with a mortar and pestle
½ cup blanched almonds, ground in a
  blender or pulverized with a mortar and
  pestle
2 tablespoons finely chopped fresh parsley
½ teaspoon ground cinnamon
Pinch of salt
2 tablespoons fresh pomegranate seeds, or
  substitute 12 pimiento strips, 2 inches
  long and ⅛ inch wide
Fresh coriander leaves

1. Whip the cream with a whisk or a rotary or electric beater until it forms soft peaks.
2. Fold in the ground nuts, parsley, ½ teaspoon of cinnamon and pinch of salt. (If you like, you may beat in a little sugar.)
3. To assemble, fill the roasted chilies with the warm beef mixture, packing it down and mounding it slightly on top.
4. Spoon the whipped cream over the top

of each pepper.
5. Scatter a teaspoon of pomegranate seeds on the cream or arrange 2 strips of pimiento over it.
6. Top with fresh coriander leaves and serve at once.

Meat Loaf with Tomatoes

To serve 5 or 6

1 medium-sized yellow onion, finely
  chopped
1 green pepper, seeded and finely chopped
3 tablespoons butter
3 thin slices white bread
1 cup light cream
1 pound ground roast beef
1 pound ground lean pork
1 egg
Salt
Pepper
¼ teaspoon oregano
3½ cups canned tomatoes

1. Preheat the oven to 350°.
2. Sauté the chopped onion and pepper in 2 tablespoons of the butter until soft but not brown.
3. Meanwhile cut the crust off the bread and put the slices into a mixing bowl.
4. Cover them with the light cream and let this mixture stand for about 5 minutes.
5. Add the ground beef, pork, egg, salt, pepper and oregano.
6. Mix the ingredients until they are thoroughly blended, adding the sautéed onion and pepper, plus about ¼ cup of the liquid from the canned tomatoes.
7. Place in a loaf pan that has been greased with the remaining butter, forming the meat so that there is a little space on each side.
8. Pour the canned tomatoes and remaining juice over the top and sides.
9. Bake uncovered in the oven for 1 hour, basting several times.
10. Serve hot or cold.

Peppers Stuffed with Beef

Dolmeh Felfel Sabz *To serve 8*

8 green peppers
2½ cups water
¼ cup dry yellow split peas
¼ cup raw rice
4 tablespoons butter
¾ cup minced yellow onions
1 pound ground beef
½ teaspoon ground cinnamon
3 teaspoons salt
¾ teaspoon pepper
¼ cup chopped green onions
3 tablespoons minced parsley
2 cups peeled chopped tomatoes
Yoghurt

1. Wash the peppers, cut a half-inch slice from the stem ends and reserve.
2. Scoop out the seeds and fibers from the peppers.
3. Cover the peppers with water, bring to a boil and cook over low heat for 5 minutes, then drain.
4. Bring 2½ cups of water to a boil. Add the split peas and rice.
5. Cook them for 25 minutes, stirring occasionally, then drain the peas and rice.
6. Melt 2 tablespoons of the butter in a skillet. Add the yellow onions and beef.
7. Cook them over medium heat for 10 minutes, stirring frequently.
8. Mix in the cinnamon, 1½ teaspoons of the salt, ½ teaspoon of the pepper, the green onions, parsley and cooked split peas and rice.
9. Stuff the peppers with this mixture and replace the reserved tops.
10. Melt the remaining butter in a deep skillet or casserole. Arrange the stuffed peppers in it in an upright position.
11. Mix the tomatoes with the remaining salt and pepper; pour over the peppers.
12. Bring to a boil, cover and cook over low heat for 35 minutes, or until the peppers are tender.
13. Top with yoghurt and serve immediately.

Veal

Veal Scallops with Prosciutto and Cheese

Cuiscinetti di Vitello   *To serve 4*

16 thin 4-inch square veal scallops
8 thin 3½-inch-square slices Fontina or
  Gruyére cheese
8 thin 3-inch-square slices prosciutto
Salt
Freshly ground black pepper
Flour
2 tablespoons butter
3 tablespoons olive oil
½ cup dry white wine
¾ cup chicken or beef stock, fresh or
  canned

1. Place a square slice of cheese and a square of prosciutto on each one of eight veal scallops and top with the remaining scallops. The veal should cover the cheese and ham completely.
2. Press the edges of the veal together and seal them by pounding with the flat of a cleaver or the bottom of a heavy bottle.
3. Season with salt and pepper; dip them in flour and shake off the excess.
4. In a heavy 10- to 12-inch skillet, melt the butter with the oil over moderate heat. When the foam subsides, add the *cuscinetti* 3 or 4 at a time and cook in the hot fat, turning gently with a slotted spoon or spatula until they are golden brown on both sides.
5. Transfer them to a platter.
6. Discard most of the fat from the skillet, leaving a thin film on the bottom.
7. Pour in the wine and boil it briskly, stirring and scraping in any browned bits that cling to the skillet.
8. Continue to boil until the wine has been reduced to about ¼ cup.
9. Add ½ cup of stock and bring it to a simmer.
10. Then return the veal to the skillet, cover, and simmer 20 minutes over low heat, turning the *cuscinetti* over after 10 minutes.
11. Transfer the *cusinetti* to a heated serving platter, and add the remaining ¼ cup of stock to the skillet.
12. Bring the stock and the pan juices to a boil, and let them cook briskly for a minute or so.
13. Taste and season with salt and pepper, then pour over the veal.

Sautéed Veal Scallops with Lemon

Scaloppine al Limone   To serve 4

**1½ pounds veal scallops, cut ⅜ inch thick
  and pounded until ¼ inch thick**
Salt
Freshly ground black pepper
Flour
2 tablespoons butter
3 tablespoons olive oil
¾ cup beef stock, fresh or canned
6 paper-thin lemon slices
1 tablespoon lemon juice
2 tablespoons soft butter

1. Season the veal scallops with salt and pepper, then dip them in flour and shake off the excess.
2. In a heavy 10- to 12-inch skillet, melt 2 tablespoons of butter with the 3 tablespoons of oil over moderate heat.
3. When the foam subsides, add the veal, 4 or 5 scallops at a time, and sauté them for about 2 minutes on each side, or until they are golden brown.
4. With tongs, transfer the veal scallops to a plate.
5. Now pour off almost all the fat from the skillet, leaving a thin film on the bottom.
6. Add ½ cup of beef stock and boil it briskly for 1 or 2 minutes, stirring constantly and scraping in any browned bits clinging to the bottom and sides of the pan.
7. Return the veal to the skillet and arrange the lemon slices on top.
8. Cover the skillet and simmer over low heat for 10 to 15 minutes, or until the veal is tender when pierced with the tip of a sharp knife.
9. To serve, transfer the scallops to a heated platter and surround with the lemon slices.
10. Add the ¼ cup of remaining beef stock to the juices in the skillet and boil briskly until the stock is reduced to a syrupy glaze.
11. Add the lemon juice and cook, stirring, for 1 minute.
12. Remove the pan from the heat, swirl in 2 teaspoons of soft butter and pour the sauce over the scallops.

Sautéed Veal Scallops with Marsala Sauce

10/86 with sherry

Scaloppine al Marsala   To serve 4

**1½ pounds veal scallops, sliced ⅜ inch
  thick and pounded to ¼ inch**
Salt
Freshly ground black pepper
Flour
2 tablespoons butter
3 tablespoons olive oil
½ cup dry Marsala
**½ cup chicken or beef stock, fresh or
  canned**
2 tablespoons soft butter

1. Season the veal scallops with salt and pepper, then dip them in flour and vigorously shake off the excess. In a heavy 10- to 12-inch skillet, melt 2 tablespoons of butter with the 3 tablespoons of oil over moderate heat.
2. When the foam subsides, add the scallops, 3 or 4 at a time, and brown them for about 3 minutes on each side.
3. Transfer them to a plate.
4. Pour off most of the fat from the skillet, leaving a thin film on the bottom.
5. Add the Marsala and ¼ cup of chicken or beef stock and boil the liquid briskly over high heat for 1 or 2 minutes.
6. Scrape in any browned fragments clinging to the bottom and sides of the pan.
7. Return the veal to the skillet, cover the pan and simmer over low heat for 10 to 15 minutes, basting the veal now and then with the pan juices.
8. To serve, transfer the scallops to a heated platter.

9. Add ¼ cup of stock to the sauce remaining in the skillet and boil briskly, scraping in the browned bits sticking to the bottom and sides of the pan.

10. When the sauce has reduced considerably, and has the consistency of a syrupy glaze, taste it for seasoning.

11. Remove the pan from the heat, stir in 2 tablespoons of soft butter, and pour the sauce over the scallops.

Sautéed Veal Scallops in Tomato Sauce

Ternera a la Sevillana — To serve 6

12 pitted green Spanish olives
1 cup olive oil
2 cups finely chopped onions
1 tablespoon finely chopped garlic
2 small green peppers, deribbed, seeded and finely chopped
¼ pound fresh mushrooms, sliced ⅛ inch thick (about 2 cups sliced)
4 medium-sized tomatoes, peeled, seeded, and finely chopped
½ cup finely diced *serrano* ham, or substitute ⅛ pound prosciutto or other lean smoked ham
2 tablespoons blanched almonds, pulverized in a blender or with a nut grinder or mortar and pestle
Salt
Freshly ground black pepper
1 cup flour
6 veal scallops, cut about ⅜ inch thick and pounded ¼ inch thick
½ cup pale dry sherry
½ cup water

1. In a small glass, enameled, or stainless-steel saucepan, bring 2 cups of water to a boil over high heat.

2. Drop in the olives, reduce the heat to low and simmer for 2 minutes.

3. Drain the olives in a sieve or colander and run cold water over them to stop their cooking. Set aside.

4. For the *sofrito*, heat ½ cup of the olive oil in a heavy 10- to 12-inch skillet over moderate heat until a light haze forms above it.

5. Add the onions, garlic and green pepper and stirring frequently, cook for 5 minutes, or until the vegetables are soft but not brown.

6. Add the mushrooms, tomatoes, olives, ham and pulverized almonds, and bring to a boil, stirring constantly.

7. Cook briskly until most of the liquid in the pan evaporates and the mixture is thick enough to hold its shape lightly in a spoon. Set aside.

8. Sprinkle the veal scallops liberally with salt and a few grindings of pepper.

9. Dip them in the flour and shake them vigorously to remove all but a light dusting.

10. Heat the remaining ½ cup of oil in another 10- to 12-inch skillet until a light haze forms above it.

11. Cook the scallops (in two batches if necessary) for 3 or 4 minutes on each side, turning them with tongs and regulating the heat so that they brown quickly and evenly without burning.

12. As they brown, transfer the scallops to a plate.

13. Discard the oil remaining in the pan and in its place pour in the sherry and water.

14. Bring to a boil over high heat, meanwhile scraping in any brown particles clinging to the bottom and sides of the skillet.

15. Then add the reserved *sofrito* and stir together thoroughly. Taste the sauce for seasoning.

16. Return the veal to the skillet, lower the heat, cover tightly and simmer for 4 or 5 minutes, or until the scallops are tender when pierced with a knife.

17. To serve, arrange the scallops attractively in a row down the center of a deep heated platter, overlapping them slightly, pour the sauce evenly over them and serve at once.

Sautéed Veal Scallops with Cream Sauce

Escalopes de Veau à la Savoyarde   To serve 4

8 veal scallops, cut ½ inch thick and
 pounded ¼ inch thick (1½ to 2 pounds)
Salt
Freshly ground black pepper
Flour
3 tablespoons butter
1 tablespoon vegetable oil
2 tablespoons finely chopped shallots or
 scallions
½ cup dry white wine
½ cup heavy cream
A few drops of lemon juice
Fresh parsley sprigs

1. Season the scallops with salt and a few grindings of pepper.
2. Dip them in flour and then shake them vigorously to remove all but a light dusting.
3. In a 10- to 12-inch enameled or stainless-steel skillet, melt the butter with the oil over moderate heat. When the foam subsides, brown the scallops for 3 or 4 minutes on each side, or until they are a light golden color.
4. Remove them from the pan and set aside.
5. Pour off almost all the fat from the skillet, leaving just enough to make a thin film on the bottom.
6. Stir in the shallots and cook at low heat for a moment.
7. Pour in the wine and bring it to a boil over high heat, stirring and scraping in any browned bits that cling to the bottom or sides of the pan.
8. Boil for 2 or 3 minutes until the wine has been reduced to about ¼ cup.
9. Reduce the heat, stir in the cream and simmer, stirring constantly, for 3 to 5 minutes, or until the sauce thickens.
10. Taste and season with a few drops of lemon juice, salt and pepper.
11. Return the scallops to the skillet, baste with the sauce and cook just long enough

to heat the scallops through.
12. Arrange the scallops, overlapping them slightly, down the center of a heated serving platter, pour the sauce over them, decorate with parsley and serve at once.

Rolled Veal Scallops with Chicken Liver Stuffing

Involtini alla Cacciatora   To serve 4 to 6

2 tablespoons butter
¼ pound chicken livers
1 ounce prosciutto, cut in tiny pieces
1 green scallion stem, finely chopped
2 teaspoons finely chopped fresh parsley
⅛ teaspoon sage leaves, crumbled
⅛ teaspoon salt
Freshly ground black pepper
1 pound veal scallops, sliced ⅜ inch thick
 and pounded ¼ inch thick, then cut into
 4-by-4-inch squares (about 12 squares)
Flour
2 tablespoons butter
3 tablespoons olive oil
½ cup dry Marsala
1 cup chicken stock, fresh or canned

1. Over moderate heat melt 2 tablespoons of butter in a heavy 8- to 10-inch skillet.
2. When the foam subsides, add the livers and cook them, turning frequently, for 4 or 5 minutes, or until they stiffen and are lightly browned.
3. Cut them into ¼-inch cubes and place them in a large bowl.
4. Sauté the prosciutto and scallions in the same skillet for about 2 minutes, adding more butter if necessary.
5. Then, with a rubber spatula, scrape them into the bowl of livers, and add the parsley, sage, salt and a few grindings of pepper.
6. Stir together gently and taste for seasoning.
7. Place about 2 tablespoons of the chicken-

liver mixture on the bottom third of each veal scallop.

8. Roll up the scallops and tie both ends with soft string.

9. Dip the rolls in flour, then shake off the excess.

10. Melt 2 tablespoons of butter with the oil in a heavy 10- to 12-inch skillet. When the foam subsides, add the veal rolls, 4 or 5 at a time, and cook over moderate heat, turning them frequently, until they are golden brown on all sides, transfering them to a plate when done.

11. Now discard almost all of the fat from the skillet, leaving a thin film on the bottom.

12. Pour in the wine and ¾ cup of chicken stock, and boil briskly for 1 or 2 minutes, scraping in any browned fragments clinging to the pan.

13. Return the veal to the skillet, reduce the heat, cover and simmer, basting once or twice with pan juices, for 15 minutes, or until the veal is tender when pierced with the tip of a sharp knife.

14. With tongs, transfer the veal to a heated serving platter.

15. Pour the remaining stock into the skillet and boil briskly, until the liquid has reduced to ½ cup and thickened slightly.

16. Pour it over the veal rolls and serve.

Veal Cutlets with Paprika and Sour Cream

Paprika Schnitzel   *To serve 4 to 6*

2 pounds leg of veal, cut into slices ¼ inch thick

1 cup fresh lemon juice
Salt
Flour
3 tablespoons lard
3 tablespoons butter
1 cup finely chopped onions
1½ tablespoons sweet Hungarian paprika
½ cup chicken stock, fresh or canned
2 tablespoons flour
1 cup sour cream

1. In a glass, stainless-steel or enameled baking dish, marinate the cutlets in the lemon juice for 1 hour, turning them every 20 minutes or so.

2. Pat them dry with paper towels, salt them, then dip them in flour and shake off the excess.

3. In a heavy 12-inch skillet, heat the lard until a light haze forms over it, then add the cutlets.

4. Over medium heat, cook them for 3 or 4 minutes on each side, or until lightly browned, using tongs to turn them.

5. Arrange them on a serving platter, cover lightly with foil, and set them in a 200° oven to keep them warm.

6. Pour off all the fat from the skillet and replace it with the butter.

7. Melt it over medium heat, then reduce the heat to low and add the onions.

8. Cook them for 8 to 10 minutes, or until they are lightly colored.

9. Remove the skillet from the heat and stir in the paprika, continuing to stir until the onions are well coated.

10. Return the skillet to medium heat and add the chicken stock.

11. Bring to a boil, stirring in any brown bits clinging to the bottom and sides of the pan.

12. In a mixing bowl, stir the 2 tablespoons of flour into the sour cream with a wire whisk.

13. Whisking constantly, add the sour-cream mixture to the stock in the skillet.

14. Simmer for 2 or 3 minutes, or until the sauce is well heated.

15. Pour the sauce over the cutlets and serve.

Breaded Veal Cutlets

Wiener Schnitzel   *To serve 4*

2 eggs
2 tablespoons water
2 pounds leg of veal, cut into slices ¼ inch thick
Salt
Freshly ground black pepper
¼ cup flour
1 cup fine bread crumbs
1½ cups lard

1. Beat the eggs with the water only long enough to combine them.
2. Sprinkle the veal slices liberally with salt and pepper, dip them in flour and shake off the excess; next dip them in the beaten eggs and finally in the bread crumbs. Gently shake any excess crumbs from the cutlets and refrigerate for at least 20 minutes.
3. Heat the lard in a heavy 12-inch skillet until a light haze forms over it, then add the cutlets.
4. Cook over medium heat 3 to 4 minutes on each side, or until they are brown, using tongs to turn them.
5. Serve immediately, garnished with lemon wedges or anchovy butter sauce.

NOTE: *Schnitzel* is common in Germany as well as Austria. To prepare a classic German version, *Schnitzel à la Holstein,* cook the cutlets as described above. Then top each cutlet with a fried egg garnished with anchovy fillets and sprinkled with a few capers. If you wish, you may surround the cutlets with small portions of several of the following: smoked salmon, caviar, crayfish tails, lobster salad, sardines in oil, mushrooms, green beans or truffles.

Veal Cutlets with Cream-and-Mushroom Sauce

Rahm Schnitzel   *To serve 4 to 6*

2 pounds veal cutlets, cut into slices ¼ inch thick
1 cup lemon juice
Salt
Freshly ground black pepper
Flour
4 tablespoons butter
4 tablespoons vegetable oil
1 cup fresh mushrooms, sliced
½ cup heavy cream

1. In a glass, stainless-steel or enameled baking dish, marinate the cutlets in the lemon juice for 1 hour, turning them every 20 minutes or so.
2. Remove them from the lemon juice and pat them dry with paper towels.
3. Salt and pepper them generously, then dip them in flour and shake off the excess.
4. In a heavy 12-inch skillet, heat the butter and oil over high heat. When the foam subsides, add the cutlets.
5. Cook them for 1 or 2 minutes on each side over high heat, using tongs to turn them.
6. Then lower the heat to medium and cook for 5 to 6 minutes longer on each side.
7. Arrange them on a platter and set them in a 200° oven to keep warm.
8. Pour off all but a thin film of fat, add the mushrooms to the skillet and cook them for 3 or 4 minutes over medium heat.
9. Pour in the cream and bring to a boil, stirring in any brown bits that cling to the pan.
10. Cook briskly until the cream thickens enough to coat a spoon lightly.
11. Taste for seasoning, then pour the sauce over the cutlets and serve.

Veal Chops with Ham-and-Parsley Dressing

Côtes de Veau à l'Ardennaise　　　　*To serve 4*

5 tablespoons butter
½ cup finely chopped onions
¼ cup finely chopped carrots
10 juniper berries
½ teaspoon dried basil
½ teaspoon salt
Freshly ground black pepper
3 tablespoons vegetable oil
4 veal loin chops, cut 1 to 1½ inches thick
1 cup dry white wine
½ cup chicken stock, fresh or canned
**¾ cup fresh white bread crumbs, made in
　a blender from about 3 slices of white
　bread with crusts removed**
1 tablespoon finely chopped boiled ham
2 tablespoons finely chopped fresh parsley
½ teaspoon lemon juice
1 tablespoon butter, cut in tiny pieces

1. Preheat the oven to 350°.
2. In a heavy shallow heatproof casserole or baking dish that is large enough to hold the chops in one layer and has a cover, melt 2 tablespoons of the butter over moderate heat, and in it cook the chopped onions and carrots, stirring occasionally, for 8 to 10 minutes or until limp and lightly colored. Set aside.
3. With a mortar and pestle or a wooden spoon and small, heavy mixing bowl, crush the juniper berries and mash in the basil, salt and a few grindings of pepper.
4. Press the juniper-berry seasoning into both sides of the chops, forcing it into the meat as much as possible.

5. Melt 1 tablespoon of the butter with the oil in a heavy 10- to 12-inch skillet over moderate heat. When the foam subsides, brown the chops to a rich golden color on both sides, turning them carefully to avoid dislodging the seasoning.
6. Transfer the browned chops to the casserole.
7. Pour off all but 1 or 2 tablespoons of fat from the skillet and add the wine.
8. Boil briskly, stirring and scraping in any browned bits that cling to the pan, until the wine has been reduced to ½ cup; then stir in the stock and pour the mixture around the veal chops.
9. In a 6- to 8-inch skillet, melt the remaining 2 tablespoons of butter over low heat, and cook the bread crumbs until they are lightly browned.
10. Off the heat, stir in the ham, parsley and ½ teaspoon of lemon juice.
11. Divide the mixture into quarters, and spoon a portion onto each chop. Dot the topping with butter.
12. Bring the casserole to a boil on top of the stove, cover tightly and bake for 40 minutes.
13. Then transfer the veal to a heated platter, preferably one with a well to catch the sauce.
14. Working quickly, strain the contents of the casserole through a fine sieve into a small saucepan, pressing down hard on the vegetables with the back of a spoon before discarding them.
15. Boil down the liquids over high heat until they are reduced to about ½ cup.
16. Taste the sauce for seasoning, pour it around the chops and serve at once.

Succulent cubes of veal and pork, divided by bay leaves, are broiled on skewers in this Serbian dish. The meat is marinated for 3 hours in oil and onions.

Veal and Pork Barbecue

Raznjići   *To serve 4 to 6*

**1 pound boneless veal, cut into 1½-inch
  cubes**
**1 pound lean boneless pork, cut into
  1½-inch cubes**
Salt
Freshly ground black pepper
2 tablespoons vegetable oil
1 cup thinly sliced onions
15 small bay leaves, broken in half
2 tablespoons finely chopped onions

1. Pat the veal and pork cubes dry with paper towels, sprinkle them with salt and a few grindings of pepper and mix them well with the oil and onions in a large bowl.
2. Cover and refrigerate for at least 3 hours, stirring them every now and then.
3. Remove the cubes to a plate and reserve the marinade for later use.
4. To prepare *raznjicí* for cooking, arrange the veal and pork cubes alternately on skewers – either small bamboo skewers or 6- to 8-inch trussing skewers – with half a bay leaf separating each pair of cubes.
5. Broil *raznjicí* in a preheated oven broiler,

4 to 6 inches from the flame, or on an outdoor grill, for 10 minutes on each side, or until the cubes show no pink in the center when one is cut into. The pork should not be undercooked.
6. With either method, baste the *raznjići* with the marinade while they are broiling.
7. *Raznjići* may be removed from the skewers before they are served, or served on the skewers.
8. Sprinkle the chopped onions over them just before serving.

Veal Chops
in Cream Sauce

Côtes de Veau à la Crème   *To serve 4*

4 veal chops
4 tablespoons butter
2 tablespoons brandy
1 small clove garlic, crushed
¼ pound mushrooms, sliced
½ teaspoon meat glaze
3 tablespoons flour
1 cup veal stock or water
1 cup heavy cream

Salt
Pepper
1 bay leaf
¼ teaspoon dried thyme
2 tablespoons grated Parmesan cheese

1. Brown the chops quickly on both sides in 2 tablespoons of hot butter.
2. Heat the brandy in a small pan, ignite it and pour it over the chops, then remove them from the pan.
3. Add 1 tablespoon of butter to the pan, then the garlic, and cook for ½ minute.
4. Add the sliced mushrooms and cook for another 2 to 3 minutes.
5. Off the heat, blend in the meat glaze and the flour.
6. Pour in the veal stock or water and stir, over the heat, until the mixture comes to a boil. Still stirring, constantly, slowly add the cream.
7. Return the chops to the sauce. Add salt and pepper to taste, the bay leaf and the thyme.
8. Cover and simmer for 40 to 50 minutes, or until the chops are tender.
9. To serve, arrange the chops on a hot, ovenproof serving dish and cover them with the sauce.
10. Sprinkle the top with Parmesan cheese and dot with the remaining tablespoon of butter, then brown under the broiler.

Casserole-roasted Veal

Veau Braisé en Casserole　　　*To serve 6*

2 tablespoons butter
2 tablespoons vegetable oil
A 3-pound boneless veal rump, shoulder or loin roast, wrapped in a thin layer of fat and tied
2 carrots, thinly sliced
2 onions, thinly sliced
½ teaspoon salt
Freshly ground black pepper
Bouquet garni made of 4 parsley sprigs and

1 bay leaf, tied together
½ teaspoon dried thyme, crumbled
½ cup hot chicken stock, fresh or canned (optional)

1. Preheat the oven to 325°.
2. In a heavy casserole that is just large enough to hold the veal and has a cover, melt the butter with the oil over moderate heat.
3. When the foam subsides, brown the veal lightly on all sides.
4. Remove the veal to a plate and stir the vegetables into the fat remaining in the casserole. (If the fat has burned, discard it and use 3 tablespoons of fresh butter instead.)
5. Cook the vegetables over low heat for 5 to 10 minutes, stirring occasionally, until they are tender but not brown.
6. Return the veal to the casserole, sprinkle it with salt and a few grindings of pepper, and the *bouquet garni* and the thyme.
7. Cover the casserole and bring it to a sizzle on top of the stove, then place it in the lower third of the oven.
8. Using a bulb baster or large spoon, baste the veal every 20 or 30 minutes with the juices that will accumulate in the pan. In the unlikely event the casserole is dry, add the hot chicken stock.
9. After 1½ hours test the veal for doneness by piercing it with the tip of a sharp knife – the juices should run clear yellow.
10. Transfer the veal to a heated platter and cut off the strings.
11. Strain the juices remaining in the casserole through a fine sieve into a small saucepan, pressing down hard on the vegetables and herbs with a spoon to extract their juices before discarding them.
12. Skim the fat from the top and boil the liquid down to about half its original volume, or until it reaches the intensity of flavor desired. Taste for seasoning.
13. Carve the veal into ¼-inch slices, moisten each slice with a little of the roasting juices and pass the rest in a warm sauceboat.

Braised Veal Shanks

Osso Buco   *To serve 6 to 8*

4 tablespoons butter
1½ cups finely chopped onions
½ cup finely chopped carrots
½ cup finely chopped celery
½ cup finely chopped garlic
6 to 7 pounds veal shank or shin, sawed—
**   not chopped—into 8 pieces, each 2½**
**   inches long, and tied with string around**
**   their circumference**
Salt
Freshly ground black pepper
Flour
½ cup olive oil
1 cup dry white wine
½ teaspoon dried basil
¾ cup beef or chicken stock, fresh or
**   canned**
½ teaspoon dried thyme
3 cups drained canned whole tomatoes,
**   coarsely chopped**
6 parsley sprigs
2 bay leaves

GREMOLATA
1 tablespoon grated lemon peel
1 teaspoon finely chopped garlic
3 tablespoons finely chopped parsley

1. Choose a heavy, shallow casserole or Dutch oven that has a tight cover and is just large enough to snugly hold the pieces of veal standing up in 1 layer.
2. Melt the butter in the casserole over moderate heat and when the foam subsides, add the chopped onions, carrots, celery and garlic.
3. Cook, stirring occasionally, for 10 to 15 minutes, or until the vegetables are lightly colored.
4. Remove the casserole from the heat.
5. Season the pieces of veal with salt and pepper, then roll them in flour and shake off the excess.
6. In a heavy 10- to 12-inch skillet, heat 6 tablespoons of olive oil until a haze forms over it.
7. Brown the veal in the oil over moderately

high heat, 4 or 5 pieces at a time, adding more oil as needed.

8. Transfer the browned pieces to the casserole and stand them side by side on top of the vegetables.

9. Preheat the oven to 350°.

10. Now discard almost all of the fat from the skillet, leaving just a film on the bottom.

11. Pour in the wine and boil it briskly over high heat until it is reduced to about ½ cup.

12. Scrape in any browned bits clinging to the pan. Stir in the beef stock, basil, thyme, tomatoes, parsley sprigs and bay leaves and bring to a boil, then pour it all over the veal. The liquid should come halfway up the side of the veal; if it does not, add more stock.

13. Bring the casserole to a boil on top of the stove.

14. Cover and bake in the lower third of the oven, basting occasionally and regulating the oven heat to keep the casserole simmering gently.

15. In about 1 hour and 15 minutes the veal should be tender; test it by piercing the meat with the tip of a sharp knife.

16. To serve, arrange the pieces of veal on a heated platter and spoon the sauce and vegetables from the casserole around them.

17. Sprinkle the top with *gremolata* – a piquant garnish made by mixing the grated lemon rind and chopped garlic and parsley together.

Veal shanks braised with vegetables, bacon and stock are served with potato dumplings and a flavorful sauce made by straining the braising liquid.

Veal Shanks with Bacon

Kalbshaxen   *To serve 4 to 6*

4 veal shanks, about 2 pounds each, sawed by the butcher into 3 or 4 pieces each
2 tablespoons butter, softened
1 cup finely chopped onions
½ cup scraped and diced parsnips
½ cup scraped and diced carrots
¼ cup coarsely chopped celery
1 bay leaf
¼ teaspoon thyme
6 peppercorns
⅛ teaspoon marjoram
⅓ cup coarsely chopped bacon
2 cups beef stock, fresh or canned
Salt

1. Preheat the oven to 500 °.
2. Using a pastry brush, thoroughly coat the shanks with the softened butter. Arrange them in a roasting pan.
3. Scatter over them the onions, parsnips, carrots, celery, bay leaf, thyme, peppercorns, marjoram and bacon.
4. Cook in the middle of the oven for about 15 minutes or until meat and vegetables are lightly browned.
5. Pour the stock (first brought to a boil in a saucepan) into the pan and scrape loose the brown bits on the sides and bottom.
6. Reduce the heat to 350°.
7. Cover the pan and cook the veal for about 1½ hours, turning it 2 or 3 times.

8. When the veal is tender, reduce the heat to 200°.

9. Arrange the shanks on a platter and return to the oven to keep warm.

10. Strain the pan juices through a fine sieve into a saucepan, pressing down hard on the vegetables with a wooden spoon before discarding them.

11. Skim off the surface fat with a large spoon, and taste.

12. If the stock seems to lack intensity of flavor, reduce it to ¾ or ½ its volume by boiling it rapidly, uncovered; then taste again for seasoning.

13. Pour the sauce over the veal shanks, or serve it separately in a sauceboat.

Marinated Veal Roast

Trouxa de Vitela   *To serve 6 to 8*

1 cup olive oil
⅓ cup white wine vinegar
1 large red onion, peeled and finely chopped
½ teaspoon finely choppped garlic

2 tablespoons finely chopped parsley
¼ teaspoon crushed dried hot red pepper
2 teaspoons salt
½ teaspoon freshly ground black pepper
A 3½- to 4-pound boneless veal roast, preferably cut from the leg or rump and securely tied

1. For the marinade, combine ¾ cup of the oil, the vinegar, onion, garlic, parsley, red pepper, salt and black pepper in a small bowl and stir well.

2. Place the veal in a deep bowl just large enough to hold it comfortably, and pour in the marinade, turning the veal about with a large spoon until it is moistened on all sides.

3. Marinate at room temperature for 4 hours or in the refrigerator for at least 8 hours, turning it over two or three times as it marinates.

4. Preheat the oven to 450°.

5. Remove the veal from the marinade, brush off any bits of onion or spice clinging to it, and place it on a rack in a shallow roasting pan.

6. Set the marinade aside in a small saucepan.

7. Roast the veal in the middle of the oven for 20 minutes. Then baste it with a tablespoon or so of olive oil and reduce the heat to 350°.

8. Basting two or three more times with the remaining olive oil, continue to roast for about 1½ hours longer, or until the veal is tender.

9. Then bring the reserved marinade to a boil over high heat, reduce the heat to low and simmer for 5 minutes.

10. To serve, carve the veal into ¼-inch slices, arrange them attractively on a large heated platter and pour the simmering marinade over them.

11. Serve at once.

A braised stuffed veal roll is combined with fresh vegetables – peas, cauliflower, carrots, leeks and green beans – to create a colorful meal.

Braised Stuffed Veal Roll

Kalbsrolle   *To serve 6 to 8*

POACHING STOCK

The bones from a leg or breast of veal,
  sawed into 2-inch lengths
4 cups water
½ cup coarsely chopped onions
½ cup coarsely chopped celery, including
  the leaves
6 whole peppercorns
1 small bay leaf

1. In a heavy 3- to 4-quart saucepan, bring the veal bones and water to a boil over high heat, skimming off any foam and scum that rise to the surface.
2. Add the ½ cup of coarsely chopped onions, the celery, peppercorns and bay leaf, reduce the heat to low and partially cover the pan.
3. Simmer, undisturbed, for 1 hour.
4. Strain the stock through a fine sieve set over a bowl, discarding the bones, vegetables and spices. Set the stock aside.

STUFFING

2 slices homemade type fresh white bread
⅓ cup milk
1 tablespoon butter
½ cup finely chopped onions
½ pound ground beef chuck
½ pound fresh sausage meat
1 egg, lightly beaten
3 tablespoons finely chopped parsley
⅛ teaspoon ground nutmeg
Salt
Freshly ground black pepper
A 4- to 4½-pound breast of veal, boned
  and trimmed
3 tablespoons lard

1. Tear the slices of bread into small pieces and soak them in the milk for 5 minutes, then gently squeeze them and set them aside in a large mixing bowl.
2. In a small skillet, melt the butter over moderate heat. When the foam subsides, add ½ cup of finely chopped onions and cook, stirring frequently, for 5 minutes, or until they are soft and transparent but not brown.
3. With a rubber spatula, scrape the contents of the skillet into the bowl with the bread, and add the beef, sausage meat, egg, parsley, nutmeg, ¼ teaspoon of salt and a few grindings of pepper.
4. Knead the mixture with your hands or beat with a large spoon until all the ingredients are well blended.
5. Preheat the oven to 325°.
6. Place the boned veal flat side down on a board or table, sprinkle it with salt and a few grindings of pepper and, with a knife or spatula, spread the ground-meat stuffing mixture evenly over the veal.
7. Beginning with a wide side, roll up the veal jelly-roll fashion into a thick cylinder.
8. Tie the roll at both ends and in the center with 8-inch lengths of white kitchen cord.
9. In a heavy flameproof casserole just large enough to hold the roll comfortably, melt the lard over high heat until a light haze forms above it.
10. Add the veal roll and brown it on all sides, regulating the heat so that it browns quickly and evenly without burning.
11. Pour in the reserved stock and bring it to a boil over high heat.
12. Cover the casserole and transfer it to the middle of the oven.
13. Cook for 1¾ hours, turning the roll over

after the first hour.

14. Then remove the cover and cook, basting occasionally with the pan juices, for 30 minutes longer, or until the veal is tender and shows no resistance when pierced with the tip of a small, sharp knife.

15. To serve hot, carve the veal into ¼-inch slices and arrange them attractively in overlapping layers on a heated platter.

16. Skim and discard the fat from the juices in the casserole, taste for seasoning, and either pour over the veal or serve separately in a sauceboat. (If you would like to make a sauce, measure the skimmed juices. If there is more than 2 cups, boil briskly to reduce it; if there is less, add water. Melt 2 tablespoons of butter over moderate heat and, when the foam subsides, stir in 3 tablespoons of flour. Cook, stirring, over low heat until the flour browns lightly. Gradually add the pan juices, beating vigorously with a whisk until the sauce is smooth and thick. Taste for seasoning.)

17. To serve cold, transfer the veal roll to a loaf pan and pour the degreased cooking juices over it.

18. Cool to room temperature, then refrigerate overnight. When cold, the juices should jell into a light aspic.

19. Serve the veal cut into thin slices.

Cold Stuffed Breast of Veal

Cima alla Genovese　　　　　　　*To serve 6 to 8*

3 slices white bread, crusts removed
⅔ cup milk
2 tablespoons butter
½ cup finely chopped onions
¼ pound boneless pork, ground twice
¼ pound boneless veal, ground twice
¼ pound fresh pork fat, ground twice
1 small calf's sweetbread, blanched 10 minutes and finely chopped
⅓ cup freshly grated imported Parmesan cheese
½ pound fresh spinach, cooked, squeezed dry and chopped, or ½ cup thoroughly squeezed and firmly packed defrosted frozen chopped spinach
¼ teaspoon dried marjoram
¼ teaspoon dried thyme
1 tablespoon salt
1 egg, lightly beaten
½ cup shelled pistachio nuts
1 cup fresh or defrosted frozen peas
A 4- to 5-pound breast of veal (ask the butcher to bone it and cut into it a pocket for stuffing)
3 hard-cooked eggs, peeled
Bones and trimmings from the breast of veal, if available
1 onion, cut in half
3 whole garlic cloves
1 carrot, peeled
1 bay leaf
2 parsley sprigs
2 to 3 quarts fresh or canned chicken stock, or water, or a combination of stock and water
Freshly ground black pepper

1. Soak the white bread in the milk for about 10 minutes.

2. Meanwhile, melt the 2 tablespoons of butter in a small skillet, and over moderate heat cook the chopped onions in the butter for 7 or 8 minutes, stirring frequently, until they are transparent but not brown.

3. Transfer the onions to a large mixing bowl, and add the ground pork, veal, pork fat, the chopped sweet-bread, grated Parmesan cheese, chopped spinach, marjoram, thyme, salt and the egg.

4. Knead all of the ingredients together with your hands or beat them with a wooden spoon until they are well mixed and fluffy.

5. Squeeze the soaked bread dry and mix it in with the other ingredients. Then gently fold in the shelled pistachio nuts and peas.

6. Spread about half of this stuffing evenly in the veal pocket and arrange the hard-cooked eggs lengthwise in a row on top of the stuffing.

7. Spoon in the rest of the stuffing, covering the eggs completely.

8. Sew up the opening of the pocket with strong kitchen thread.

9. Place the veal bones and trimmings (if available), onion halves, garlic cloves, carrot, bay leaf and parsley in a large soup pot or kettle and lay the stuffed veal on top of them.

10. Add enough stock or water to cover the meat completely, and grind in a little black pepper.

11. Bring to a boil, reduce the heat, cover the pot and simmer as gently as possible for 1¼ hours, or until the veal is tender when pierced with the tip of a sharp knife.

12. Transfer the stuffed veal to a large, heavy, shallow baking dish and let it cool to room temperature.

13. Then place the dish in the refrigerator until the meat is thoroughly chilled.

14. Serve cold, cut into ¼-inch slices.

A boned breast of veal is stuffed with ground meats, pistachio nuts, peas and hard-cooked eggs. The veal is braised, then thoroughly chilled before serving.

Cold Veal with Tuna Sauce

Vitello Tonnato   *To serve 6 to 8*

A 3- to 3½ pound boneless veal roast, securely tied
3 flat anchovy fillets, cut into 1-inch lengths
1 to 2 garlic cloves, cut into thin slivers
1 quart chicken stock, fresh or canned
2 cups dry white wine
2 cups water
2 onions, quartered
2 carrots, cut up
3 celery stalks, cut up
2 bay leaves
6 parsley sprigs
10 whole peppercorns

1. With a small sharp knife, make deep incisions along the length of the veal and insert a 1-inch piece of anchovy and a sliver of garlic in each one.
2. Blanch the veal in a large pot by covering it with cold water and boiling it over high heat for 1 minute.
3. Pour off the water and quickly rinse the meat of its scum in cold water.
4. Place the veal in a heavy saucepan or pot just large enough to hold it comfortably.
5. Add the chicken stock, wine, water, onions, carrots, celery, bay leaves, parsley and peppercorns. If the liquid does not quite cover the meat completely, add more chicken stock or water.
6. Bring to a boil, reduce the heat and simmer the veal slowly, partially covered, for about 1 hour and 40 minutes, or until the veal is tender when pierced with the tip of a sharp knife.
7. Remove the pan from the heat and let the veal cool in the stock.
8. Ladle out about ½ cup of the stock, strain it through a fine sieve, and set it aside in a cup or bowl to cool.

TUNA SAUCE
¾ cup olive oil
1 egg yolk
1 three-ounce can tuna fish, preferably Italian tuna packed in olive oil
4 flat anchovy fillets, drained and soaked in water for 10 minutes, then cut into small pieces
2 tablespoons lemon juice
¼ cup heavy cream
¼ to ½ cup cooled, strained veal-braising stock *(from above)*
2 tablespoons capers, thoroughly washed and drained
Salt
White pepper

1. Meanwhile, prepare the tuna sauce.
2. If you have a blender, all you need to do is to combine all of the olive oil, the egg yolk, tuna fish, 4 anchovy fillets and lemon juice in the jar of the blender and whirl the ingredients at high speed for about 10 seconds, or until the mixture is a purée.
3. Transfer it to a small mixing bowl and stir in the cream gradually. Add the cooled, strained braising stock from the veal 2 tablespoons at a time until the sauce is thinned to the consistency of heavy cream. You probably will need about 4 tablespoons of the braising stock in all.
4. Stir in the capers. Taste the sauce for seasoning.
5. When the veal is cool, transfer it to a carving board.
6. Strain the braising stock and refrigerate for use in soups or sauces.
7. Trim the veal of any fat or gristle and cut the meat into thin, even slices.
8. Spread a thin film of tuna sauce in the bottom of a large platter or baking dish and arrange the veal in the sauce, laying the slices side by side.
9. Pour the rest of the sauce over the veal, smoothing it with a spatula to mask each slice.
10. Cover the platter with plastic wrap and

Black olives, parsley, capers and lemon slices adorn this dish of cold veal in creamy tuna fish sauce. It may be refrigerated overnight before serving.

refrigerate the *vitello tonnato* for at least 2 or 3 hours – overnight, or longer, if possible.

GARNISH
2 tablespoons finely chopped fresh parsley, preferably the flat-leaf Italian type
2 lemons, sliced
2 tablespoons capers
12 lemons, sliced
2 tablespoons capers
12 black olives, preferably Mediterranean style

1. About 1 hour before serving, remove the veal from the refrigerator and allow it to come to room temperature.
2. Arrange the slices so that they overlap as neatly as possible in a circle on a large serving platter.
3. Spoon all of the sauce over them.
4. Sprinkle the veal and sauce with the chopped parsley, and garnish the platter with lemon slices, capers and black olives.

INDEX

PICTURE CREDITS The sources for the illustrations which appear in this book are: Cover – Richard Jeffery. 10, 12, 13 – Mark Kauffman. 17 – Henry Groskinsky. 18 – Milton Greene. 22 – Mark Kauffman. 24 – Richard Jeffery. 26 – Anthony Blake. 31 – Bill Helms. 32 – Milton Greene. 33 – Clayton Price. 37 – Fred Lyon from Rapho Guillumette. 45, 46 – Eliot Elisofan. 50 – Henry Groskinsky. 53 – Richard Jeffery. 54 – Constantine Manos from Magnum. 66, 69, 70 – Fred Lyon from Rapho Guillumette. 72 – Henry Groskinsky. 75 – Charles Phillips. 77 – Fred Lyon from Rapho Guillumette.

RECIPE CREDITS The following books were used as sources for the listed pages: *The Dione Lucas Meat and Poultry Cook Book* by Dione Lucas and Ann Roe Robbins, ©1955 by Little, Brown – 15, 21, 29, 35, 55, 66 (right). *The Embassy Cookbook* by Allison Williams ©1966 by Little, Brown – 56.

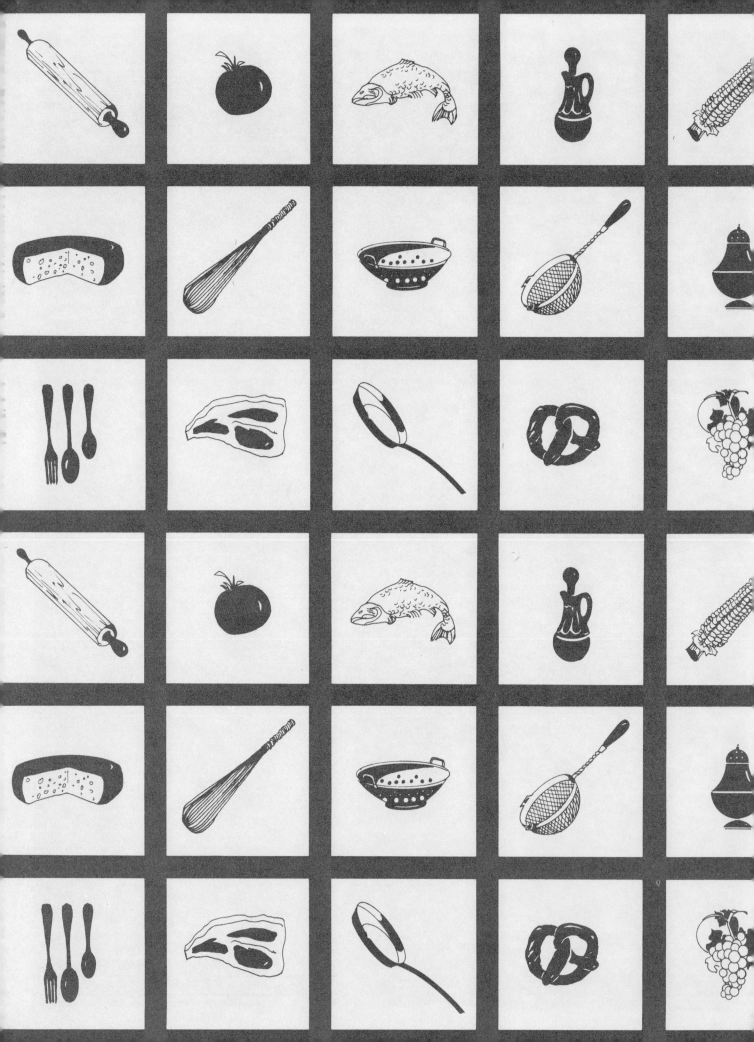